# STORIES OF GREAT AMERICANS FOR LITTLE AMERICANS

By EDWARD EGGLESTON

Stories of Great Americans for Little Americans
By Edward Eggleston

Print ISBN 13: 978-1-4209-7327-3
eBook ISBN 13: 978-1-4209-7390-7

This edition copyright © 2021. Digireads.com Publishing.

All rights reserved. No part of this publication may be reproduced, distributed, or transmitted in any form or by any means, including photocopying, recording, or other electronic or mechanical methods, without the prior written permission of the publisher, except in the case of brief quotations embodied in critical reviews and certain other noncommercial uses permitted by copyright law.

Cover Image: a detail of "Franklin's experiment in electricity", c. 1746, published by Currier and Ives (print) / Alamy Stock Photo.

Please visit *www.digireads.com*

## CONTENTS

PREFACE. .................................................................................. 7
THE FIRST GOVERNOR IN BOSTON. ................................... 8
MARQUETTE IN IOWA. ........................................................... 9
INDIAN PICTURES. ................................................................ 11
WILLIAM PENN AND THE INDIANS. .................................. 12
ONE LITTLE BAG OF RICE. ................................................. 14
THE STORY OF A WISE WOMAN. ........................................ 16
FRANKLIN HIS OWN TEACHER. ......................................... 17
HOW FRANKLIN FOUND OUT THINGS. ............................ 19
FRANKLIN ASKS THE SUNSHINE SOMETHING. .............. 22
FRANKLIN AND THE KITE. .................................................. 22
FRANKLIN'S WHISTLE. ......................................................... 25
TOO MUCH FOR THE WHISTLE. ......................................... 25
JOHN STARK AND THE INDIANS. ....................................... 26
A GREAT GOOD MAN. .......................................................... 28
PUTNAM AND THE WOLF. ................................................... 31
WASHINGTON AND HIS HATCHET. ................................... 34
HOW BENNY WEST LEARNED TO BE A PAINTER. .......... 36
WASHINGTON'S CHRISTMAS GIFT. ................................... 39
HOW WASHINGTON GOT OUT OF A TRAP. ...................... 41
WASHINGTON'S LAST BATTLE. .......................................... 43
MARION'S TOWER. ............................................................... 44
CLARK AND HIS MEN. .......................................................... 46
DANIEL BOONE AND HIS GRAPEVINE SWING. ............... 48
DANIEL BOONE'S DAUGHTER AND HER FRIENDS. ....... 50
DECATUR AND THE PIRATES. ............................................ 52

| | |
|---|---|
| STORIES ABOUT JEFFERSON. | 54 |
| A LONG JOURNEY. | 55 |
| CAPTAIN CLARK'S BURNING GLASS. | 57 |
| QUICKSILVER BOB. | 59 |
| THE FIRST STEAMBOAT. | 61 |
| WASHINGTON IRVING AS A BOY. | 62 |
| DON'T GIVE UP THE SHIP. | 65 |
| GRANDFATHER'S RHYME. | 65 |
| THE STAR-SPANGLED BANNER. | 66 |
| HOW AUDUBON CAME TO KNOW ABOUT BIRDS. | 69 |
| AUDUBON IN THE WILD WOODS. | 71 |
| HUNTING A PANTHER. | 72 |
| SOME BOYS WHO BECAME AUTHORS. | 73 |
| DANIEL WEBSTER AND HIS BROTHER. | 77 |
| WEBSTER AND THE POOR WOMAN. | 79 |
| THE INDIA-RUBBER MAN. | 79 |
| DOCTOR KANE IN THE FROZEN SEA. | 81 |
| DOCTOR KANE GETS OUT OF THE FROZEN SEA. | 84 |
| LONGFELLOW AS A BOY. | 85 |
| KIT CARSON AND THE BEARS. | 87 |
| HORACE GREELEY AS A BOY. | 89 |
| HORACE GREELEY LEARNING TO PRINT. | 91 |
| A WONDERFUL WOMAN. | 93 |
| THE AUTHOR OF "LITTLE WOMEN." | 94 |
| MY KINGDOM. | 95 |
| A SONG FROM THE SUDS. | 96 |

Burning of the "Philadelphia."

## Preface.

The primary aim of this book is to furnish the little learner reading matter that will excite his attention and give him pleasure, and thus make lighter the difficult task of learning to read. The ruggedness of this task has often been increased by the use of disconnected sentences, or lessons as dry and uninteresting as finger exercises on the piano. It is a sign of promise that the demand for reading matter of interest to the child has come from teachers. I have endeavored to meet this requirement in the following stories.

As far as possible the words chosen have been such as are not difficult to the little reader, either from their length or their unfamiliarity. The sentences and paragraphs are short. Learning to read is like climbing a steep hill, and it is a great relief to the panting child to find frequent breathing places.

It is one of the purposes of these stories to make the mind of the pupil familiar with some of the leading figures in the history of our country by means of personal anecdote. Some of the stories are those that every American child ought to know, because they have become a kind of national folklore. Such, for example, are "Putnam and the Wolf" and the story of "Franklin's Whistle." I have thought it important to present as great a variety of subjects as possible, so that the pupil may learn something not only of great warriors and patriots, but also of great statesmen. The exploits of discoverers, the triumphs of American inventors, and the achievements of men of letters and men of science, find place in these stories. All the narratives are historical, or at least no stories have been told for true that are deemed fictitious. Every means which the writer's literary experience could suggest has been used to make the stories engaging, in the hope that the interest of the narrative may prove a sufficient spur to exertion on the part of the pupil, and that this little book will make green and pleasant a pathway that has so often been dry and laborious. It will surely serve to excite an early interest in our national history by giving some of the great personages of that history a place among the heroes that impress the susceptible imagination of a child. It is thus that biographical and historical incidents acquire something of the vitality of folk tales.

The illustrations that accompany the text have been planned with special reference to the awakening of the child's attention. To keep the mind alert and at its best is more than half the battle in teaching. The publishers and the author of this little book believe that in laying the foundation of a child's education the best work is none too good.

The larger words have been divided by hyphens when a separation into syllables is likely to help the learner. The use of the hyphen has been regulated entirely with a view to its utility. After a word not too difficult has been made familiar by its repeated occurrence, the hyphens are omitted.

## The First Governor in Boston.

Before the white people came, there were no houses in this country but the little huts of the In-di-ans. The In-di-an houses were made of bark, or mats, or skins, spread over poles.

Some people came to one part of the country. Others started set-tle-ments in other places. When more people came, some of these set-tle-ments grew into towns. The woods were cut down. Farms were planted. Roads were made. But it took many years for the country to fill with people.

The first white people that came to live in the woods where Boston is now, settled there a long time ago. They had a gov-ern-or over them. He was a good man, and did much for the people. His name was John Win-throp.

The first thing the people had to do was to cut down the trees. After that they could plant corn. But at first they could not raise any-thing to eat. They had brought flour and oat-meal from England. But they found that it was not enough to last till they could raise corn on their new ground.

Win-throp sent a ship to get more food for them. The ship was gone a long time. The people ate up all their food. They were hungry. They went to the sea-shore, and found clams and mussels. They were glad to get these to eat.

At last they set a day for every-body to fast and pray for food. The gov-ern-or had a little flour left. Nearly all of this was made into bread, and put into the oven to bake. He did not know when he would get any more.

Soon after this a poor man came along. His flour was all gone. His bread had all been eaten up. His family were hungry. The gov-ern-or gave the poor man the very last flour that he had in the barrel.

Just then a ship was seen. It sailed up toward Boston. It was loaded with food for all the people.

The time for the fast day came. But there was now plenty of food. The fast day was turned into a thanks-giving day.

One day a man sent a very cross letter to Gov-ern-or Win-throp. Win-throp sent it back to him. He said, "I cannot keep a letter that might make me angry." Then the man that had written the cross letter wrote to Win-throp, "By con-quer-ing yourself, you have con-quered me."

### Marquette in Iowa.

The first white men to go into the middle of our country were French-men. The French had settled in Can-a-da. They sent mis-sion-a-ries to preach to the Indians in the West. They also sent traders to buy furs from the Indians.

The French-men heard the Indians talk about a great river in the West. But no French-man had ever gone far enough to see the Mis-sis-sip-pi.

Mar-quette was a priest. Jo-li-et was a trader. These two men were sent to find the great river that the Indians talked about.

They trav-eled in two birch canoes. They took five men to paddle the canoes. They took some smoked meat to eat on the way. They also took some Indian corn. They had trinkets to trade to the Indians. Hatchets, and beads, and bits of cloth were the money they used to pay the Indians for what they wanted.

The friendly Indians in Wis-con-sin tried to per-suade them not to go. They told them that the Indians on the great river would kill them.

The friendly Indians also told them that there was a demon in one part of the river. They said that this demon roared so loud that he could be heard a long way off. They said that the demon would draw the trav-el-ers down into the water. Then they told about great monsters that ate up men and their canoes.

But Mar-quette and the men with him thought they would risk the journey. They would not turn back for fear of the demon or the monsters.

The two little canoes went down the Wis-con-sin River. After some days they came to the Mis-sis-sip-pi. More than a hundred years before, the Spaniards had seen the lower part of this river. But no white man had ever seen this part of the great river. Mar-quette did not know that any white man had ever seen any part of the Mis-sis-sip-pi.

The two little canoes now turned their bows down the river. Sometimes they saw great herds of buf-fa-loes. Some of these came to the bank of the river to look at the men in the canoes. They had long, shaggy manes, which hung down over their eyes.

For two weeks the trav-el-ers paddled down the river. In all this time they did not see any Indians. After they had gone hundreds of miles in this way, they came to a place where they saw tracks in the mud. It was in what is now the State of I-o-wa.

Mar-quette and Jo-li-et left the men in their canoes, and followed the tracks. After walking two hours, they came to an Indian village. The Frenchmen came near enough to hear the Indians talking. The Indians did not see them.

Jo-li-et and Mar-quette did not know whether the Indians would kill them or not. They said a short prayer. Then they stood out in full view, and gave a loud shout.

The Indians came out of their tents like bees. They stared at the strangers. Then four Indians came toward them. These Indians carried a peace pipe. They held this up toward the sun. This meant that they were friendly.

The Indians now offered the peace pipe to the French-men. The French-men took it, and smoked with the Indians. This was the Indian way of saying, "We are friends."

Marquette and Joliet.

Mar-quette asked the Indians what tribe they belonged to. They told him that they were of the tribe called the Il-li-nois.

They took Jo-li-et and Mar-quette into their village. They came to the door of a large wig-wam. A chief stood in the door. He shaded his

*Edward Eggleston*

eyes with both hands, as if the sun were shining in his face. Then he made a little speech.

He said, "French-men, how bright the sun shines when you come to see us! We are all waiting for you. You shall now come into our houses in peace."

The Il-li-nois Indians made a feast for their new friends. First they had mush of corn meal, with fat meat in it. One of the Indians fed the Frenchmen as though they were babies. He put mush into their mouths with a large spoon.

Then came some fish. The Indian that fed the vis-it-ors picked out the bones with his fingers. Then he put the pieces of fish into their mouths. After they had some roasted dog. The French-men did not like this. Last, they were fed with buf-fa-lo meat.

The next morning six hundred Indians went to the canoes to tell the Frenchmen good-by. They gave Mar-quette a young Indian slave. And they gave him a peace pipe to carry with him.

*Indian Pictures.*

When Mar-quette and his men left the Il-li-nois, they went on down the river. The friendly Il-li-nois had told them that the Indians they would see were bad, and that they would kill any one who came into their country.

The Frenchmen had heard before this that there were demons and monsters in the river. One day they saw some high rocks with pictures painted on them. The ugly pictures made them think of these monsters. They were painted in red, black, and green colors. They were pictures of two Indian demons or gods.

Each one of these monsters was about the size of a calf. They had horns as long as those of a deer. Their eyes were red. Their faces were like a man's, but they were ugly and frightful. They had beards like a tiger's. Their bodies were covered with scales like those on a fish. Their long tails were wound round their bodies, and over their heads, and down between their legs. The end of each tail was like that of a fish.

The Indians prayed to these ugly gods when they passed in their canoes. Even Mar-quette and his men were a little frightened when they saw such pictures in a place so lonely.

The Frenchmen went down the river about twelve hundred miles. Some-times the Indians tried to kill them, but by showing the peace pipe they made friends. At last they turned back. Jo-li-et went to Can-a-da. Mar-quette preached to the Indians in the West till he died.

## William Penn and the Indians.

The King of England gave all the land in Penn-syl-va-ni-a to William Penn. The King made Penn a kind of king over Penn-syl-va-ni-a. Penn could make the laws of this new country. But he let the people make their own laws.

Penn wanted to be friendly with the Indians. He paid them for all the land his people wanted to live on. Before he went to Penn-syl-va-ni-a he wrote a letter to the Indians. He told them in this letter that he would not let any of his people do any harm to the Indians. He said he would punish any-body that did any wrong to an Indian. This letter was read to the Indians in their own lan-guage.

Soon after this Penn got into a ship and sailed from England. He sailed to Penn-syl-va-ni-a. When he came there, he sent word to the tribes of Indians to come to meet him.

The Indians met under a great elm tree on the bank of the river. Indians like to hold their solemn meetings out of doors. They sit on the ground. They say that the earth is the Indian's mother.

When Penn came to the place of meeting, he found the woods full of Indians. As far as he could see, there were crowds of Indians. Penn's friends were few. They had no guns.

Penn had a bright blue sash round his waist. One of the Indian chiefs, who was the great chief, put on a kind of cap or crown. In the middle of this was a small horn. The head chief wore this only at such great meetings as this one.

When the great chief had put on his horn, all the other chiefs and great men of the Indians put down their guns. Then they sat down in front of Penn in the form of a half-moon. Then the great chief told Penn that the Indians were ready to hear what he had to say.

Penn had a large paper in which he had written all the things that he and his friends had promised to the Indians. He had written all the promises that the Indians were to make to the white people. This was to make them friends. When Penn had read this to them, it was explained to them in their own lan-guage. Penn told them that they might stay in the country that they had sold to the white people. The land would belong to both the Indians and the white people.

Then Penn laid the large paper down on the ground. That was to show them, he said, that the ground was to belong to the Indians and the white people to-geth-er.

He said that there might be quarrels between some of the white people and some of the Indians. But they would settle any quarrels without fighting. When-ever there should be a quarrel, the Indians were to pick out six Indians. The white people should also pick out six of their men. These were to meet, and settle the quarrel.

Penn said, "I will not call you my children, because fathers sometimes whip their children. I will not call you brothers, because brothers sometimes fall out. But I will call you the same person as the white people. We are the two parts of the same body."

The Indians could not write. But they had their way of putting down things that they wished to have re-mem-bered. They gave Penn a belt of shell beads. These beads are called wam-pum. Some wam-pum is white. Some is purple.

They made this belt for Penn of white beads. In the middle of the belt they made a picture of purple beads. It is a picture of a white man and an Indian. They have hold of each other's hands. When they gave this belt to Penn, they said, "We will live with William Penn and his children as long as the sun and moon shall last."

Penn jumping with the Indians.

Penn took up the great paper from the ground. He handed it to the great chief that wore the horn on his head. He told the Indians to keep it and hand it to their children's children, that they might know what he had said. Then he gave them many presents of such things as they liked.

They gave Penn a name in their own language. They named him "O-nas." That was their word for a feather. As the white people used a pen made out of a quill or feather, they called a pen "o-nas." That is why they called William Penn "Brother O-nas."

Penn sometimes went to see the Indians. He talked to them, and gave them friendly advice. Once he saw some of them jumping. They were trying to see who could jump the farthest.

Penn had been a very active boy. He knew how to jump very well. He went to the place where the Indians were jumping. He jumped farther than any of them.

When the great gov-ern-or took part in their sport, the Indians were pleased. They loved Brother O-nas more than ever.

### *One Little Bag of Rice*

The first white people that came to this country hardly knew how to get their living here. They did not know what would grow best in this country.

Many of the white people learned to hunt. All the land was covered with trees. In the woods were many animals whose flesh was good to eat.

There were deer, and bears, and great shaggy buf-fa-loes. There were rabbits and squirrels. And there were many kinds of birds. The hunters shot wild ducks, wild turkeys, wild geese, and pigeons. The people also caught many fishes out of the rivers.

Then there were animals with fur on their backs. The people killed these and sold their skins. In this way many made their living.

Other people spent their time in cutting down the trees. They sawed the trees into timbers and boards. Some of it they split into staves to make barrels. They sent the staves and other sorts of timber to other countries to be sold. In South Car-o-li-na men made tar and pitch out of the pine trees.

But there was a wise man in South Car-o-li-na. He was one of those men that find out better ways of doing. His name was Thomas Smith.

Thomas Smith had once lived in a large island thousands of miles away from South Car-o-li-na. In that island he had seen the people raising rice. He saw that it was planted in wet ground. He said that he would like to try it in South Car-o-li-na. But he could not get any seed rice to plant. The rice that people eat is not fit to sow.

One day a ship came to Charles-ton, where Thomas Smith lived. It had been driven there by storms. The ship came from the large island where Smith had seen rice grow. The captain of this ship was an old friend of Smith.

The two old friends met once more. Thomas Smith told the captain that he wanted some rice for seed. The captain called the cook of his ship, and asked him if he had any. The cook had one little bag of seed rice. The captain gave this to his friend.

There was some wet ground at the back of Smith's garden. In this wet ground he sowed some of the rice. It grew finely.

Rice Plant.

He gathered a good deal of rice in his garden that year. He gave part of this to his friends. They all sowed it. The next year there was a great deal of rice.

After a while the wet land in South Car-o-li-na was turned to rice fields. Every year many thousands of barrels of rice were sent away to be sold.

All this came from one little bag of rice and one wise man.

## The Story of a Wise Woman.

You have read how Thomas Smith first raised rice in Car-o-li-na. After his death there lived in South Car-o-li-na a wise young woman. She showed the people how to raise another plant. Her name was Eliza Lucas.

The father of Miss Lucas did not live in Car-o-li-na. He was gov-ern-or of one of the islands of the West Indies. Miss Lucas was fond of trying new things. She often got seeds from her father. These she planted in South Carolina.

Her father sent her some seeds of the in-di-go plant. She sowed some of these in March. But there came a frost. The in-di-go plant cannot stand frost. Her plants all died.

But Miss Lucas did not give up. She sowed some more seeds in April. These grew very well until a cut-worm found them. The worm wished to try new things, too. So he ate off the in-di-go plants.

But Miss Lucas was one of the people who try, try again. She had lost her indigo plants twice. Once more she sowed some of the seed. This time the plants grew very well.

Miss Lucas wrote to her father about it. He sent her a man who knew how to get the indigo out of the plant.

The man tried not to show Miss Lucas how to make the indigo. He did not wish the people in South Carolina to learn how to make it. He was afraid his own people would not get so much for their indigo.

So he would not explain just how it ought to be done. He spoiled the indigo on purpose.

But Miss Lucas watched him closely. She found out how the indigo ought to be made. Some of her father's land in South Carolina was now planted with the indigo plants.

Then Miss Lucas was married. She became Mrs. Pinck-ney. Her father gave her all the indigo growing on his land in South Carolina. It was all saved for seed. Some of the seed Mrs. Pinck-ney gave to her friends. Some of it her husband sowed. It all grew, and was made into that blue dye that we call indigo. When it is used in washing clothes, it is called bluing.

In a few years, more than a million pounds of indigo were made in South Carolina every year. Many people got rich by it. And it was all because Miss Lucas did not give up.

*Edward Eggleston* 17

Indigo Plant.

*Franklin His Own Teacher.*

    Few people ever knew so many things as Franklin. Men said, "How did he ever learn so many things?" For he had been a poor boy who had to work for a living. He could not go to school at all after he was ten years old.

    His father made soap and candles. Little Ben Frank-lin had to cut wicks for the candles. He also filled the candle molds. And he sold soap and candles, and ran on errands. But when he was not at work he spent his time in reading good books. What little money he got he used to buy books with.

    He read the old story of "Pil-grim's Prog-ress," and liked it so well that he bought all the other stories by the same man. But as he wanted more books, and had not money to buy them, he sold all of these books. The next he bought were some little his-to-ry books. These were made to sell very cheap, and they were sold by peddlers. He managed to buy forty or fifty of these little books of his-to-ry.

Another way that he had of learning was by seeing things with his own eyes. His father took him to see car-pen-ters at work with their saws and planes. He also saw masons laying bricks. And he went to see men making brass and copper kettles. And he saw a man with a turning lathe making the round legs of chairs. Other men were at work making knives. Some things people learn out of books, and some things they have to see for them-selves.

Franklin at Study.

*Edward Eggleston*

As he was fond of books, Ben's father thought that it would be a good plan to send him to learn to print them. So the boy went to work in his brother's printing office. Here he passed his spare time in reading. He borrowed some books out of the stores where books were sold. He would sit up a great part of the night sometimes to read one of these books. He wished to return it when the book-store opened in the morning. One man who had many books lent to Ben such of his books as he wanted.

It was part of the bargain that Ben's brother should pay his board. The boy offered to board himself if his brother would give him half what it cost to pay for his board.

His brother was glad to do this, and Ben saved part of the money and bought books with it. He was a healthy boy, and it did not hurt him to live mostly on bread and butter. Sometimes he bought a little pie or a handful of raisins.

Long before he was a man, people said, "How much the boy knows!" This was because—

He did not waste his time.

He read good books.

He saw things for himself.

### *How Franklin Found Out Things.*

Frank-lin thought that ants know how to tell things to one another. He thought that they talk by some kind of signs. When an ant has found a dead fly too big for him to drag away, he will run off and get some other ant to help him. Frank-lin thought that ants have some way of telling other ants that there is work to do.

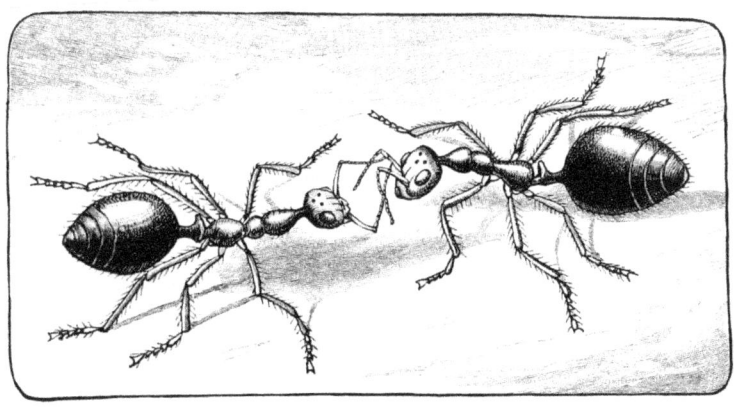

Ants talking (magnified).

One day he found some ants eating mo-las-ses out of a little jar in a closet. He shook them out. Then he tied a string to the jar, and hung it on a nail in the ceiling. But he had not got all the ants out of the jar. One little ant liked sweet things so well that he staid in the jar, and kept on eating like a greedy boy.

At last when this greedy ant had eaten all that he could, he started to go home. Frank-lin saw him climb over the rim of the jar. Then the ant ran down the outside of the jar. But when he got to the bottom, he did not find any shelf there. He went all round the jar. There was no way to get down to the floor. The ant ran this way and that way, but he could not get down.

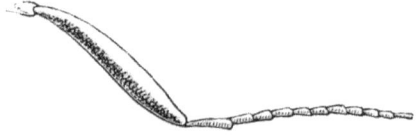

An Ants Feeler (magnified).

At last the greedy ant thought he would see if he could go up. He climbed up the string to the ceiling. Then he went down the wall. He came to his own hole at last, no doubt.

After a while he got hungry again, perhaps. He thought about that jar of sweets at the end of a string. Then perhaps he told the other ants. Maybe he let them know that there was a string by which they could get down to the jar.

In about half an hour after the ant had gone up the string, Franklin saw a swarm of ants going down the string. They marched in a line, one after another. Soon there were two lines of ants on the string. The ants in one line were going down to get at the sweet food. The ants in the other line were marching up the other side of the string to go home. Do you think that the greedy ant told the other ants about the jar?

And did he tell them that there was a string by which an ant could get there? And did he tell it by speaking, or by signs that he made with his feelers?

If you watch two ants when they meet, you will see that they touch their feelers together, as if they said "Good-morning!"

### Franklin Asks the Sunshine Something.

One day Franklin was eating dinner at the house of a friend. The lady of the house, when she poured out the coffee, found that it was not hot.

She said, "I am sorry that the coffee is cold. It is because the servant forgot to scour the coffee-pot. Coffee gets cold more quickly when the coffee-pot is not bright."

This set Franklin to thinking. He thought that a black or dull thing would cool more quickly than a white or bright one. That made him think that a black thing would take in heat more quickly than a white one.

He wanted to find out if this were true or not. There was no-body who knew, so there was no-body to ask. But Franklin thought that he would ask the sunshine. Maybe the sunshine would tell him whether a black thing would heat more quickly than a white thing.

But how could he ask the sunshine?

There was snow on the ground. Franklin spread a white cloth on the snow. Then he spread a black cloth on the snow near the white one. When he came to look at them, he saw that the snow under the black cloth melted away much sooner than that under the white cloth.

That is the way that the sunshine told him that black would take in heat more quickly than white. After he had found this out, many people got white hats to wear in the summer time. A white hat is cooler than a black one.

Some time when there is snow on the ground, you can take a white and a black cloth and ask the sunshine the same question.

### Franklin and the Kite.

When Franklin wanted to know whether the ants could talk or not, he asked the ants, and they told him. When he wanted to know something else, he asked the sunshine about it, as you have read in another story. That is the way that Franklin came to know so many things. He knew how to ask questions of every-thing.

Once he asked the light-ning a question. And the light-ning gave him an answer.

Before the time of Franklin, people did not know what light-ning was. They did not know what made the thunder. Franklin thought much about it. At last he proved what it was. He asked the lightning a question, and made it tell what it was. To tell you this story, I shall have to use one big word. Maybe it is too big for some of my little friends that will read this book. Let us divide it into parts. Then you will not be afraid of it. The big word is e-lec-tric-i-ty.

Franklin's Discovery.

Those of you who live in towns have seen the streets lighted by e-lec-tric-i-ty. But in Franklin's time there were no such lights. People knew very little about this strange thing with a big name.

But Franklin found out many things about it that nobody had ever known before. He began to think that the little sparks he got from e-lec-tric-i-ty were small flashes of lightning. He thought that the little cracking sound of these sparks was a kind of baby thunder.

So he thought that he would try to catch a little bit of lightning. Perhaps he could put it into one of the little bottles used to hold e-lec-tric-i-ty. Then if it behaved like e-lec-tric-i-ty, he would know what it was. But catching lightning is not easy. How do you think he did it?

First he made a kite. It was not a kite just like a boy's kite. He wanted a kite that would fly when it rained. Rain would spoil a paper kite in a minute. So Franklin used a silk hand-ker-chief to cover his kite, instead of paper.

He put a little sharp-pointed wire at the top of his kite. This was a kind of lightning rod to draw the lightning into the kite. His kite string was a common hemp string. To this he tied a key, because lightning will follow metal. The end of the string that he held in his hand was a silk ribbon, which was tied to the hemp string of the kite. E-lec-tric-ity will not follow silk.

One night when there was a storm coming, he went out with his son. They stood under a cow shed, and he sent his kite up in the air.

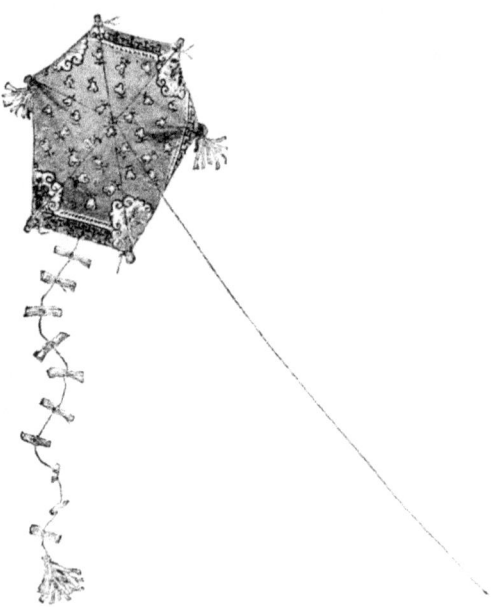

After a while he held his knuckle to the key. A tiny spark flashed between the key and his knuckle. It was a little flash of lightning.

Then he took his little bottle fixed to hold e-lec-tric-i-ty. He filled it with the e-lec-tric-i-ty that came from the key. He carried home a bottle of lightning. So he found out what made it thunder and lighten.

After that he used to bring the lightning into his house on rods and

*Edward Eggleston* 25

wires. He made the lightning ring bells and do many other strange things.

### Franklin's Whistle.

When Franklin was an old man, he wrote a cu-ri-ous letter. In that letter he told a story. It was about some-thing that happened to him when he was a boy.

Here is the story put into verses, so that you will re-member it better. Some day you can read the story as Franklin told it himself. You will hear people say, "He paid too much for the whistle." The saying came from this story.

### Too Much For the Whistle.

As Ben with pennies in his pocket
  Went strolling down the street,
"Toot-toot! toot-toot!" there came a whistle
  From a boy he chanced to meet,

Whistling fit to burst his buttons,
   Blowing hard and stepping high.
Then Benny said, "I'll buy your whistle;"
   But "Toot! toot-toot!" was the reply.

But Benny counted out his pennies,
   The whistling boy began to smile;
With one last toot he gave the whistle
   To Ben, and took his penny pile.

Now homeward goes the whistling Benny,
   As proud as any foolish boy,
And in his pockets not a penny,
   But in his mouth a noisy toy.

"Ah, Benny, Benny!" cries his mother,
   "I cannot stand your ugly noise."
"Stop, Benny, Benny!" says his father,
   "I cannot talk, you drown my voice."

At last the whistling boy re-mem-bers
   How much his money might have bought
"Too many pennies for a whistle,"
   Is little Benny's ugly thought.

Too many pennies for a whistle
   Is what we all pay, you and I,
Just for a little foolish pleasure
   Pay a price that's quite too high.

### *John Stark and the Indians.*

    John Stark was a famous gen-er-al in the Rev-o-lu-tion. But this story is not about the Rev-o-lu-tion. It is about Stark before he became a soldier.

    When he was a young man, Stark went into the woods. His brother and two other young men were with him. They lived in a camp. It was far away from any houses.

    The young men set traps for animals in many places. They wanted to catch the animals that have fur on them. They wanted to get the skins to sell.

    The Indians were at war with the white people. One day the young men saw the tracks of Indians. Then they knew that it was not safe for them to stay in the woods any longer. They began to get ready to go home.

John Stark went out to bring in the traps set for animals. The Indians found him, and made him a pris-on-er. They asked him where his friends were.

Stark did not wish his friends to be taken. So he pointed the wrong way. He took the Indians a long way from the other young men.

But John Stark's friends did not know that he was a pris-on-er. When he did not come back, they thought that he had lost his way. They fired their guns to let him know where they were.

When the Indians heard the guns, they knew where the other hunters were. They went down to the river, and waited for them. When one of the men came down, they caught him.

Then John Stark's brother and the other man came down the river in a boat. The Indians told Stark to call them. They wanted them to come over where the Indians were. Then they could take them.

John knew that the Indians were cruel. He knew that if he did not do what they told him to, they might kill him. But he wished to save his brother. He called to his brother to row for the other shore.

When they turned toward the other shore, the Indians fired at them. But Stark knocked up two of their guns. They did not hit the white men. Then some of the other Indians fired. Stark knocked up their guns also. But the man that was with his brother was killed.

John now called to his brother, "Run! for all the Indians' guns are empty."

His brother got away. The Indians were very angry with John. They did not kill him. But they gave him a good beating.

Stark running the Gauntlet.

These Indians were from Can-a-da. They took their pris-on-ers to their own village. When they were coming home, they shouted to let the people know that they had prisoners.

The young Indian war-ri-ors stood in two rows in the village. Each prisoner had to run between these two rows of Indians. As he passed, every one of the Indians hit him as hard as he could with a stick, or a club, or a stone.

The young man who was with Stark was badly hurt in running between these lines. But John Stark knew the Indians. He knew that they liked a brave man.

When it came his turn to run, he snatched a club from one of the Indians. With this club he fought his way down the lines. He hit hard, now on this side, and now on that. The young Indians got out of his way. The old Indians who were looking on sat and laughed at the others. They said that Stark was a brave man.

One day the Indians gave him a hoe and told him to hoe corn. He knew that the Indian war-ri-ors would not work. They think it a shame for a man to work. Their work is left for slaves and women. So Stark pre-tend-ed that he did not know how to hoe. He dug up the corn instead of the weeds. Then he threw the hoe into the river.

He said, "That is work for slaves and women."

Then the Indians were pleased with him. They called him the young chief.

After a while some white men paid the Indians a hundred and three dollars to let Stark go home. They charged more for him than for the other man, because they thought that he must be a young chief. Stark went hunting again. He had to get some furs to pay back the money the men had paid the Indians for him. He took good care that the Indians should not catch him again.

He af-ter-wards became a great fighter against the Indians. He had learned their ways while he was among them. He knew better how to fight them than almost any-body else.

In the Rev-o-lu-tion he was a gen-er-al. He fought the British at Ben-ning-ton, and won a great vic-to-ry.

## A Great Good Man.

Some men are great soldiers. Some are great law-makers. Some men write great books. Some men make great in-ven-tions. Some men are great speakers.

Now you are going to read about a man that was great in none of these things. He was not a soldier. He was not a great speaker. He was never rich. He was a poor school-teacher. He never held any office.

And yet he was a great man. He was great for his goodness.

He was born in France. But most of his life was passed in Phil-a-del-phi-a before the Rev-o-lu-tion.

He was twenty-five years old when he became a school-teacher. He thought that he could do more good in teaching than in any other way.

School-masters in his time were not like our teachers. Children were treated like little animals. In old times the school-master was a little king. He walked and talked as if he knew every-thing. He wanted all the children to be afraid of him.

But Ben-e-zet was not that kind of man. He was very gentle. He treated the children more kindly than their fathers and mothers did. Nobody in this country had ever seen a teacher like him.

He built a play-room for the children of his school. He used to take them to this room during school time for a little a-muse-ment. He managed each child as he found best. Some he could persuade to be good. Some he shamed into being good. But this was very dif-fer-ent from the cruel beatings that other teachers of that time gave their pupils.

Of course the children came to love him very much. After they grew to be men and women, they kept their love for the good little schoolmaster. As long as they lived they listened to his advice.

There were no good school-books in his time. He wrote some little books to make learning easier to his pupils. He taught them many things not in their books. He taught them to be kind to brutes, and gentle with one another. He taught them to be noble. He made them despise every kind of meanness.

He was a great teacher. That is better than being a great soldier.

Ben-e-zet was a good man in many ways. He was the friend of all poor people. Once he found a poor man suf-fer-ing with cold for want of a coat. He took off his own coat in the street and put it on the poor man, and then went home in his shirt sleeves.

In those days negroes were stolen from Af-ri-ca to be sold into A-mer-i-ca. Ben-e-zet wrote little books against this wrong. He sent these books over all the world almost. He also tried to persuade the white men of his own country to be honest and kind with the Indians.

Great men in other countries were pleased with his books. They wrote him letters. When any of them came to this country, they went to see him. They wanted to see a man that was good to everybody. His house was a plain one. But great men liked to sit at the table of the good schoolmaster.

There was war between the English and French at that time. Can-a-da belonged to the French. Our country belonged to the English. There was a country called A-ca-di-a. It was a part of what is now No-va Sco-ti-a. The people of A-ca-di-a were French.

The English took the A-ca-di-ans away from their homes. They sent them to various places. Many families were divided. The poor A-ca-di-ans lost their homes and all that they had.

Many hundreds of these people were sent to Phil-a-del-phi-a. Benezet became their friend. As he was born in France, he could speak their lan-guage. He got a large house built for some of them to stay in. He got food and clothing for them. He helped them to get work, and did them good in many other ways.

Departure of the Acadians.

One day Benezet's wife came to him with a troubled face. She said, "There have been thieves in the house. Two of my blankets have been stolen."

"Never mind, my dear," said Benezet, "I gave them to some of the poor A-ca-di-ans."

One old Acadian was afraid of Benezet. He did not see why Benezet should take so much trouble for other people. He thought that Benezet was only trying to get a chance to sell the Acadians for slaves. When Benezet heard this, he had a good laugh.

Many years after this the Rev-o-lu-tion broke out. It brought trouble to many people. Benezet helped as many as he could.

After a while the British army took Phil-a-del-phi-a. They sent their soldiers to stay in the houses of the people. The people had to take care of the soldiers. This was very hard for the poor people.

One day Benezet saw a poor woman. Her face showed that she was in trouble.

"Friend, what is the matter?" Benezet said to her.

She told him that six soldiers of the British army had been sent to stay in her house. She was a washer-woman. But while the soldiers filled up the house she could not do any washing. She and her children were in want.

Benezet went right away to see the gen-er-al that was in command of the soldiers. The good man was in such a hurry that he forgot to get a pass. The soldiers at the gen-er-al's door would not let him go in.

At last some one told the gen-er-al that a queer-looking fellow wanted to see him.

"Let him come up," said the general.

The odd little man came in. He told the general all about the troubles of the poor washer-woman. The general sent word that the soldiers must not stay any longer in her house.

The general liked the kind little man. He told him to come to see him again. He told the soldiers at his door to let Benezet come in whenever he wished to.

Soon after the Rev-o-lu-tion was over, Benezet was taken ill. When the people of Phil-a-del-phi-a heard that he was ill, they gathered in crowds about his house. Every-body loved him. Every-body wanted to know whether he was better or not. At last the doctors said he could not get well. Then the people wished to see the good man once more. The doors were opened. The rooms and halls of his house were filled with people coming to say good-bye to Benezet, and going away again.

When he was buried, it seemed as if all Phil-a-del-phi-a had come to his fu-ner-al. The rich and the poor, the black and the white, crowded the streets. The city had never seen so great a fu-ner-al.

In the company was an A-mer-i-can general. He said, "I would rather be An-tho-ny Benezet in that coffin than General Wash-ing-ton in all his glory."

## Putnam and the Wolf.

Putnam was a brave soldier. He fought many battles against the Indians. After that he became a general in the Revolution. But this is a story of his battle with a wolf. It took place when he was a young man, before he was a soldier.

Putnam lived in Con-nect-i-cut. In the woods there were still a few wolves. One old wolf came to Putnam's neigh-bor-hood every winter. She always brought a family of young wolves with her.

The hunters would always kill the young wolves. But they could not find the old mother wolf. She knew how to keep out of the way.

The farmers tried to catch her in their traps. But she was too cunning. She had had one good lesson when she was young. She had put the toes of one foot into a steel trap. The trap had snipped them off. After that she was more careful.

One winter night she went out to get some meat. She came to

Putnam's flock of sheep and goats. She killed some of them. She found it great fun.

There were no dogs about. The poor sheep had nobody to protect them. So the old wolf kept on killing. One sheep was enough for her supper. But she killed the rest just for sport. She killed seventy sheep and goats that night.

Putnam and his friends set out to find the old sheep killer. There were six men of them. They agreed that two of them should hunt for her at a time. Then another two should begin as soon as the first two should stop. So she would be hunted day and night.

The hunters found her track in the snow. There could be no mistake about it. The track made by one of her feet was shorter than those made by the other feet. That was because one of her feet had been caught in a trap.

The hunters found that the old wolf had gone a long way off. Perhaps she felt guilty. She must have thought that she would be hunted. She had trotted away for a whole night.

Then she turned and went back again. She was getting hungry by this time. She wanted some more sheep.

The men followed her tracks back again. The dogs drove her into a hole. It was not far from Putnam's house.

All the farmers came to help catch her. They sent the dogs into the cave where the wolf was. But the wolf bit the dogs, and drove them out again.

Then the men put a pile of straw in the mouth of the cave. They set the straw on fire. It filled the cave with smoke. But Mrs. Wolf did not come out.

Then they burned brim-stone in the cave. It must have made the wolf sneeze. But the cave was deep. She went as far in as she could, and staid there. She thought that the smell of brimstone was not so bad as the dogs and men who wanted to kill her.

Putnam wanted to send his negro into the cave to drive out the wolf. But the negro thought that he would rather stay out.

Then Putnam said that he would go in himself. He tied a rope to his legs. Then he got some pieces of birch-bark. He set fire to these. He knew that wild animals do not like to face a fire.

He got down on his hands and knees. He held the blazing bark in his hand. He crawled through the small hole into the cave. There was not room for him to stand up.

At first the cave went downward into the ground. Then it was level a little way. Then it went upward. At the very back of this part of the cave was the wolf. Putnam crawled up until he could see the wolf's eyes.

When the wolf saw the fire, she gave a sudden growl. Putnam jerked the rope that was tied to his leg. The men outside thought that the wolf had caught him. They pulled on the other end of the rope.

The men pulled as fast as they could. When they had drawn Putnam out, his clothes were torn. He was badly scratched by the rocks.

He now got his gun. He held it in one hand. He held the burning birch-bark in the other. He crawled into the cave again.

When the wolf saw him coming again, she was very angry. She snapped her teeth. She got ready to spring on him. She meant to kill him as she had killed his sheep. Putnam fired at her head. As soon as his gun went off, he jerked the rope. His friends pulled him out.

He waited awhile for the smoke of his gun to clear up. Then he went in once more. He wanted to see if the wolf was dead.

He found her lying down. He tapped her nose with his birch-bark. She did not move. He took hold of her. Then he jerked the rope.

This time the men saw him come out, bringing the dead wolf. Now the sheep would have some peace.

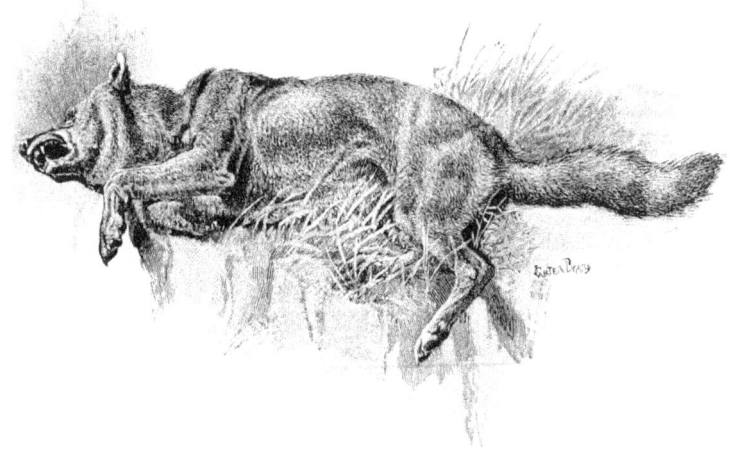

*Washington and His Hatchet.*

## WASHINGTON AND HIS HATCHET.

It was Ar-bor Day in the Mos-sy Hill School, and Johnny Little-john had to speak a piece that had some-thing to do with trees. He thought it would be a good plan to say some-thing about the little cherry tree that Washington spoiled with his hatch-et when he was a little boy. This is what he said:

He had a hatch-et — little George —
    A hatch-et bright and new,
And sharp enough to cut a stick —
    A little stick — in two.

He hacked and whacked and whacked
    and hacked,
    This sturd-y little man;
He hacked a log and hacked a fence,
    As round about he ran.

He hacked his father's cher-ry tree
    And made an ug-ly spot;
The bark was soft, the hatch-et sharp,
    And little George forgot.

You know the rest. The father frowned
  And asked the rea-son why;
You know the good old story runs.
  He could not tell a lie.

The boy that chopped that cher-ry tree
  Soon grew to be a youth;
At work and books he hacked away,
  And still he told the truth.

The youth became a fa-mous man,
  Above six feet in height,
And when he had good work to do
  He hacked with all his might.

He fought the ar-mies that the king
  Had sent across the sea;
He bat-tled up and down the land
  To set his country free.

For seven long years he hacked and
    whacked
  With all his might and main,
Until the Brit-ish sailed away
  And did not come again.

## How Benny West Learned to Be a Painter.

In old times there lived in Penn-syl-va-ni-a a little fellow whose name was Ben-ja-min West. He lived in a long stone house.

Painting Baby's Portrait.

He had never seen a picture. The country was new, and there were not many pictures in it. Benny's father was a Friend or Quaker. The Friends of that day did not think that pictures were useful things to make or to have.

Before he was seven years old, this little boy began to draw pictures. One day he was watching the cradle of his sister's child. The baby smiled. Benny was so pleased with her beauty, that he made a picture of her in red and black ink. The picture of the baby pleased his mother when she saw it. That was very pleasant to the boy.

He made other pictures. At school he used to draw with a pen before he could write. He made pictures of birds and of animals. Sometimes he would draw flowers.

He liked to draw so well, that sometimes he forgot to do his work. His father sent him to work in the field one day. The father went out to see how well he was doing his work. Benny was no-where to be found. At last his father saw him sitting under a large poke-weed. He was making pictures. He had squeezed the juice out of some poke-berries. The juice of poke-berries is deep red. With this the boy had made his pictures. When the father looked at them, he was surprised. There were portraits of every member of the family. His father knew every picture.

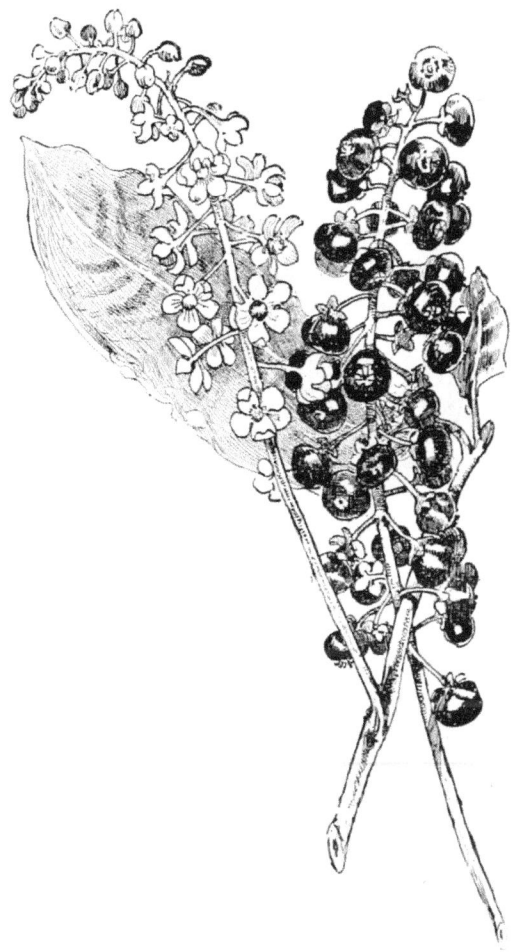

Flower and Fruit of the Poke-Berry.

Up to this time Benny had no paints nor any brushes. The Indians had not all gone away from that neigh-bor-hood. The Indians paint their faces with red and yellow colors. These colors they make them-selves. Sometimes they prepare them from the juice of some plant. Sometimes they get them by finding red or yellow earth. Some of the Indians can make rough pictures with these colors.

The Indians near the house of Benny's father must have liked the boy. They showed him how to make red and yellow colors for himself.

He got some of his mother's indigo to make blue. He now had red, yellow, and blue. By mixing these three, the other colors that he wanted could be made.

But he had no brush to paint with. He took some long hairs from the cat's tail. Of these he made his brushes. He used so many of the cat's hairs, that her tail began to look bare. Everybody in the house began to wonder what was the matter with pussy's tail. At last Benny told where he got his brushes.

Making a Paint Brush.

A cousin of Benny's came from the city on a visit. He saw some of the boy's drawings. When he went home, he sent Benny a box of paints. With the paints were some brushes. And there was some canvas such as pictures are painted on. And that was not all. There were in the box six beautiful en-grav-ings.

The little painter now felt himself rich. He was so happy that he could hardly sleep at all. At night he put the box that held his treasures on a chair by his bed. As soon as daylight came, he carried the precious box to the garret. The garret of the long stone house was his stu-di-o. Here he worked away all day long. He did not go to school at all. Perhaps he forgot that there was any school. Perhaps the little artist could not tear himself away from his work.

But the schoolmaster missed him. He came to ask if Benny was ill. The mother was vexed when she found that he had staid away from school. She went to look for the naughty boy. After a while she found the little truant. He was hard at work in his garret. She saw what he had been doing. He had not copied any of his new en-grav-ings. He had made up a new picture by taking one person out of one en-grav-ing, and another out of another. He had copied these so that they made a picture that he had thought of for himself.

His mother could not find it in her heart to punish him. She was too much pleased with the picture he was making. This picture was not finished. But his mother would not let him finish it. She was afraid he would spoil it if he did anything more on it.

The good people called Friends did not like the making of pictures, as I said. But they thought that Benny West had a talent that he ought to use. So he went to Phil-a-del-phi-a to study his art. After a while he sailed away to It-a-ly to see the pictures that great artists had painted.

At last he settled in England. The King of England was at that time the king of this country too. The king liked West's pictures. West became the king's painter. He came to be the most famous painter in England.

He liked to remember his boyish work. He liked to remember the time when he was a little Quaker boy making his paints of poke-juice and Indian colors.

### Washington's Christmas Gift.

Washington was fighting to set this country free. But the army that the King of England sent to fight him was stronger than Washington's army. Washington was beaten and driven out of Brook-lyn. Then he had to leave New York. After that, he marched away into New Jersey to save his army from being taken. At last he crossed the Del-a-ware River. Here he was safe for a while.

Some of the Hes-sian soldiers that the king had hired to fight against the Americans came to Trenton. Trenton is on the Del-a-ware River.

Washington and his men were on the other side of the Del-a-ware River from the Hes-sians. Washington's men were dis-cour-aged. They had been driven back all the way from Brook-lyn. It was winter, and they had no warm houses to stay in. They had not even warm clothes. They were dressed in old clothes that people had given them. Some of them were bare-footed in this cold weather.

The Hes-sians and other soldiers of the king were waiting for the river to freeze over. Then they would march across on the ice. They meant to fight Washington once more, and break up his army. But Washington was thinking about something too.

He was waiting for Christmas. He knew that the Hessian soldiers on the other side of the river would eat and drink a great deal on Christmas Day.

The afternoon of Christmas came. The Hessians were singing and drinking in Trenton. But Washington was marching up the river bank. Some of his bare-foot men left blood marks on the snow as they marched.

The men and cannons were put into flat boats. These boats were pushed across the river with poles. There were many great pieces of ice in the river. But all night long the flat boats were pushed across and then back again for more men.

It was three o'clock on the morning after Christmas when the last Americans crossed the river. It was hailing and snowing, and it was very cold. Two or three of the soldiers were frozen to death.

Marching to Trenton.

It was eight o'clock in the morning when Washington got to Trenton. The Hessians were sleeping soundly. The sound of the American drums waked them. They jumped out of their beds. They ran into the streets. They tried to fight the Americans.

But it was too late. Washington had already taken their cannons. His men were firing these at the Hessians. The Hessians ran into the fields to get away. But the Americans caught them.

The battle was soon over. Washington had taken nine hundred prisoners.

This was called the battle of Trenton. It gave great joy to all the Americans. It was Washington's Christmas gift to the country.

*Edward Eggleston*

## *How Washington Got Out of a Trap.*

After the battle of Trenton, Washington went back across the Delaware River. He had not men enough to fight the whole British army.

But the Americans were glad when they heard that he had beaten the Hessians. They sent him more soldiers. Then he went back across the river to Trenton again.

There was a British general named Corn-wal-lis. He marched to Trenton. He fought against Washington. Corn-wal-lis had more men than Washington had. Night came, and they could not see to fight. There was a little creek between the two armies.

Washington had not boats enough to carry his men across the river. Corn-wal-lis was sure to beat him if they should fight a battle the next morning.

Cornwallis said, "I will catch the fox in the morning."

He called Washington a fox. He thought he had him in a trap. Cornwallis sent for some more soldiers to come from Prince-ton in the morning. He wanted them to help him catch the fox.

But foxes sometimes get out of traps.

When it was dark, Washington had all his camp fires lighted. He put men to digging where the British could hear them. He made Cornwallis think that he was throwing up banks of earth and getting ready to fight in the morning.

But Washington did not stay in Trenton. He did not wish to be caught like a fox in a trap. He could not get across the river. But he knew a road that went round the place where Cornwallis and his army were. He took that road and got behind the British army.

It was just like John waiting to catch James. James is in the house. John is waiting at the front door to catch James when he comes out. But James slips out by the back way. John hears him call "Hello!" James has gone round behind him and got away.

Washington went out of Trenton in the darkness. You might say that he marched out by the back door. He left Cornwallis watching the front door. The Americans went away quietly. They left a few men to keep up the fires, and make a noise like digging. Before morning these slipped away too.

When morning came, Cornwallis went to catch his fox. But the fox was not there.

He looked for the Americans. There was the place where they had been digging. Their camp fires were still burning. But where had they gone?

Cornwallis thought that Washington had crossed the river by some means. But soon he heard guns firing away back toward Princeton. He thought that it must be thunder. But he found that it was a battle. Then he knew that Washington had gone to Princeton.

Washington had marched all night. When he got to Princeton, he met the British coming out to go to Trenton. They were going to help Cornwallis to catch Washington. But Washington had come to Princeton to catch them. He had a hard fight with the British at Princeton. But at last he beat them.

When Cornwallis knew that the Americans had gone to Princeton, he hurried there to help his men. But it was too late. Washington had beaten the British at Princeton, and had gone on into the hills, where he was safe.

The fox had got out of the trap.

## Washington's Last Battle.

Washington had been fighting for seven years to drive the British soldiers out of this country. But there were still two strong British armies in America.

One of these armies was in New York. It had been there for years. The other army was far away at Yorktown in Virginia. The British general at Yorktown was Cornwallis. You have read how Washington got away from him at Trenton.

The King of France had sent ships and soldiers to help the Americans. But still Washington had not enough men to take New York from the British. Yet he went on getting ready to attack the British in New York. He had ovens built to bake bread for his men. He bought hay for his horses. He had roads built to draw his cannons on.

He knew that the British in New York would hear about what he was doing. He wanted them to think that he meant to come to New York and fight them. When the British heard what the Americans were doing, they got ready for the coming of Washington and the French.

All at once they found that Washington had gone. He and his men had marched away. The French soldiers that had come to help him had gone with him.

Nobody knew what it meant. Washington's own men did not know where they were going. They went from New Jersey into Penn-syl-va-ni-a. Then they marched across Penn-syl-va-ni-a. Then they went into Mary-land. They marched across that State, and then they went into Vir-gin-i-a.

By this time everybody could tell where Washington was going. People could see that he was going straight to York-town. They knew that Washington was going to fight his old enemy at York-town.

But he had kept his secret long enough. The British in New York could not send help to Cornwallis. It was too late. The French ships sailed to Vir-gin-i-a, and shut up Yorktown on the side of the sea. Washington's men shut it up on the side of the land. They built great banks of earth round it. On these banks of earth they put cannons.

The British could not get away. They fought bravely. But the Americans and French came closer and closer.

Then the British tried to fight their way out. But they were driven back. Then Cornwallis tried to get his men across the river. He wanted to get out by the back door, as Washington had done. But the Americans on the other side of the river drove them back again. Washington had now caught Cornwallis in a trap.

The Americans fired red-hot cannon balls into Yorktown. These set the houses on fire. At last Cornwallis had to give up. The British marched out and laid down their guns and swords.

The British army in New York could not fight the Americans by itself. So the British gave it up. Then there was peace after the long war. The British pulled down the British flag and sailed away. The country was free at last.

## Marion's Tower.

General Mar-i-on was one of the best fighters in the Revolution. He was a homely little man. He was also a very good man. Another general said, "Mar-i-on is good all over."

The American army had been beaten in South Car-o-li-na. Mar-i-on was sent there to keep the British from taking the whole country.

Marion got to-geth-er a little army. His men had nothing but rough clothes to wear. They had no guns but the old ones they had used to shoot wild ducks and deer with.

Marion's men wanted swords. There were no swords to be had. But Marion sent men to take the long saws out of the saw mills. These were taken to black-smiths. The black-smiths cut the saws into pieces. These pieces they hammered out into long, sharp swords.

Marion had not so many men as the British. He had no cannon. He could not build forts. He could not stay long in one place, for fear the British should come with a strong army and take him. He and his men hid in the dark woods. Sometimes he changed his hiding place suddenly. Even his own friends had hard work to find him.

From the dark woods he would come out suddenly. He would attack some party of British soldiers. When the battle was over, he would go back to the woods again.

When the British sent a strong army to catch him, he could not be found. But soon he would be fighting the British in some new place. He was always playing hide and seek.

The British called him the Swamp Fox. That was because he was so hard to catch. They could not conquer the country until they could catch Marion. And they never could catch the Swamp Fox.

At one time Marion came out of the woods to take a little British fort. This fort was on the top of a high mound. It was one of the mounds built a long time ago by the Indians.

Marion put his men all round the fort, so that the men in the fort could not get out to get water. He thought that they would have to give up. But the men in the fort dug a well inside the fort. Then Marion had to think of another plan.

Marion's men went to the woods and cut down stout poles. They got a great many poles. When night came, they laid a row of poles along-side one another on the ground. Then they laid another row across these. Then they laid another row on top of the last ones, and across the other way again.

Marion's Tower.

They laid a great many rows of poles one on top of another. They crossed them this way and that. As the night went on, the pile grew higher. Still they handed poles to top of the pile.

Before morning came, they had built a kind of tower. It was higher than the Indian mound.

As soon as it was light, the men on Marion's tower began to shoot. The British looked out. They saw a great tower with men on it. The men could shoot down into the fort. The British could not stand it. They had to give up. They were taken prisoners.

## Clark and His Men.

At the time of the Revolution there were but few people living on the north side of the O-hi-o River. But there were many Indians there. These Indians killed a great many white people in Ken-tuck-y. The Indians were sent by British officers to do this killing. There was a British fort at Vincennes in what is now In-di-an-a. There was another British fort or post at Kas-kas-ki-a in what is now the State of Il-li-nois.

George Rogers Clark was an American colonel. He wanted to stop the murder of the settlers by the Indians. He thought that he could do it by taking the British posts.

He had three hundred men. They went down the O-hi-o River in boats. They landed near the mouth of the O-hi-o River. Then they marched a hundred and thirty miles to Kas-kas-ki-a.

Kas-kas-ki-a was far away from the Americans. The people there did not think that the Americans would come so far to attack them. When Clark got there, they were all asleep. He marched in and took the town before they waked up.

The people living in Kaskaskia were French. By treating them well, Clark made them all friendly to the Americans.

When the British at Vin-cennes heard that Clark had taken Kaskaskia, they thought that they would take it back again. But it was winter. All the streams were full of water. They could not march till spring. Then they would gather the Indians to help them, and take Clark and his men.

But Clark thought that he would not wait to be taken. He thought that he would just go and take the British. If he could manage to get to Vin-cennes in the winter, he would not be expected.

Clark started with a hundred and seventy men. The country was nearly all covered with water. The men were in the wet almost all the time. Clark had hard work to keep his men cheerful. He did everything he could to amuse them.

They had to wade through deep rivers. The water was icy cold. But Clark made a joke of it. He kept them laughing whenever he could.

At one place the men refused to go through the freezing water. Clark could not per-suade them to cross the river. He called to him a tall sol-dier. He was the very tallest man in Clark's little army. Clark said to him, "Take the little drummer boy on your shoulders."

The little drummer was soon seated high on the shoulders of the tall man. "Now go ahead!" said Clark.

The soldier marched into the water. The little drummer beat a march on his drum. Clark cried out, "Forward!" Then he plunged into the water after the tall soldier. All the men went in after him. They were soon safe on the other side.

At another river the little drummer was floated over on the top of his drum.

At last the men drew near to Vin-cennes. They could hear the morning and evening gun in the British fort. But the worst of the way was yet to pass. The Wa-bash River had risen over its banks. The water was five miles wide. The men marched from one high ground to another through the cold water. They caught an Indian with a canoe. In this they got across the main river. But there was more water to cross. The men were so hungry that some of them fell down in the water. They had to be carried out.

Clark's men got frightened at last, and then they had no heart to go any farther. But Clark remembered what the Indians did when they went to war. He took a little gun-powder in his hand. He poured water on it. Then he rubbed it on his face. It made his face black.

With his face blackened like an Indian's, he gave an Indian war-whoop.

The men followed him again. The men were tired and hungry. But they soon reached dry ground. They were now in sight of the fort. Clark marched his little army round and round in such a way as to make it seem that he had many men with him. He wrote a fierce letter to the British com-mand-er. He behaved like a general with a large army.

After some fighting, the British com-mand-er gave up. Clark's little army took the British fort. This brave action saved to our country the land that lies between the Ohio River and the Lakes. It stopped the sending of Indians to kill the settlers in the West.

### Daniel Boone and His Grapevine Swing.

Daniel Boone was the first settler of Ken-tuck-y. He knew all about living in the woods. He knew how to hunt the wild animals. He knew how to fight Indians, and how to get away from them.

Nearly all the men that came with him to Kentucky the first time were killed. One was eaten by wolves. Some of them were killed by Indians. Some of them went into the woods and never came back. Nobody knows what killed them.

Only Boone and his brother were left alive. They needed some powder and some bullets. They wanted some horses. Boone's brother went back across the mountains to get these things. Boone staid in his little cabin all alone.

Boone could hear the wolves howl near his cabin at night. He heard the panthers scream in the woods. But he did not mind being left all alone in these dark forests.

The Indians came to his cabin when he was away. He did not want to see these vis-it-ors. He did not dare to sleep in his cabin all the time. Sometimes he slept under a rocky cliff. Sometimes he slept in a cane-brake. A cane-brake is a large patch of growing canes such as fishing rods are made of.

Once a mother bear tried to kill him. He fired his gun at her, but the bullet did not kill her. The bear ran at him. He held his long knife out in his hand. The bear ran against it and was killed.

He made long journeys alone in the woods. One day he looked back through the trees and saw four Indians. They were fol-low-ing Boone's tracks. They did not see him. He turned this way and that. But the Indians still fol-lowed his tracks.

He went over a little hill. Here he found a wild grape-vine. It was a very long vine, reaching to the top of a high tree. There are many such vines in the Southern woods. Children cut such vines off near the roots. Then they use them for swings.

Boone had swung on grape-vines when he was a boy. He now

thought of a way to break his tracks. He cut the wild grape-vine off near the root. Then he took hold of it. He sprang out into the air with all his might. The great swing carried him far out as it swung. Then he let go. He fell to the ground, and then he ran away in a dif-fer-ent di-rec-tion from that in which he had been going.

When the Indians came to the place, they could not find his tracks. They could not tell which way he had gone. He got to his cabin in safety.

Boone had now been alone for many months. His brother did not get back at the time he had set for coming. Boone thought that his brother might have been killed. Boone had not tasted anything but meat since he left home. He had to get his food by shooting animals in the woods. By this time he had hardly any powder or bullets left.

Boone on the Grapevine Swing.

One evening he sat by his cabin. He heard some one coming. He thought that it might be Indians. He heard the steps of horses. He looked through the trees. He saw his brother riding on one horse, and leading another. The other horse was loaded with powder and bullets and clothes, and other things that Boone needed.

*Daniel Boone's Daughter and Her Friends.*

Daniel Boone and his brother picked out a good place in Ken-tuck-y to settle. Then they went home to North Car-o-li-na. They took with them such things as were cu-ri-ous and val-u-a-ble. These were the skins of animals they had killed, and no doubt some of the heads and tails.

Boone was restless. He had seen Kentucky and he did not wish to settle down to the life of North Carolina.

In two years Boone sold his farm in North Carolina and set out for Kentucky. He took with him his wife and children and two brothers. Some of their neighbors went with them. They trav-eled by pack train. All their goods were packed on horses.

When they reached the place on the Kentucky River that Boone had chosen for a home they built a fort of log houses. These cabins all stood round a square. The backs of the houses were outward. There was no door or window in the back of a house. The outer walls were thus shut up. They made the place a fort. The houses at the four corners were a little taller and stronger than the others.

There were gates leading into the fort. These gates were kept shut at night.

In the evening the people danced and amused themselves in the square. Indians could not creep up and attack them.

When the men went out to feed the horses and cows they carried their guns. They walked softly and turned their eyes quickly from point to point to see if Indians were hiding near. They held their guns so they could shoot quickly.

The women and children had to stay very near the fort so they could run in if an Indian came in sight.

Daniel Boone had a daughter named Je-mi-ma. She was about fourteen years old. She had two friends named Frances and Betsey Cal-lo-way. Frances Galloway was about the same age as Jemima.

One summer afternoon these three girls went out of the fort. They went to the river and got into a canoe. It was not far from the fort. They felt safe. They laughed and talked and splashed the water with their paddles.

The cur-rent carried them slowly near the other shore. They could still see the fort. They did not think of danger.

Trees and bushes grew thick down to the edge of the river. Five strong Indians were hiding in the bushes.

One Indian crept care-ful-ly through the bushes. He made no more noise than a snake. When he got to the edge of the water he put out his long arm and caught hold of the rope that hung down from the canoe. In a moment he had turned the boat around and drawn it out of sight from the fort. The girls screamed when they saw the Indian. Their friends heard them but could not cross the river to help them. The girls had taken the only canoe.

Boone and Cal-lo-way were both gone from the fort. They got home too late to start that day. No sleep came to their eyes while they waited for light to travel by.

Boone and Calloway saved.

As soon as there was a glim-mer of light they and a party of their friends set out. It was in July and they could start early.

They crossed the river and easily found the Indians' tracks where they started. The brush was broken down there.

The Indians were cun-ning. They did not keep close together after they set out. Each Indian walked by himself through the tall canes. Three of the Indians took the captives.

Boone and his friends tried in vain to follow them. Sometimes they would find a track but it would soon be lost in the thick canes.

Boone's party gave up trying to find their path. They noticed which way the Indians were going. Then they walked as fast as they could the same way for thirty miles. They thought the Indians would grow careless about their tracks after traveling so far.

They turned so as to cross the path they thought the Indians had taken. They looked carefully at the ground and at the bushes to see if any one had gone by.

Before long they found the Indians' tracks in a buffalo path.

Buffaloes and other animals go often to lick salt from the rocks round salt springs. They beat down the brush and make great roads. These roads run to the salt springs. The hunters call them streets.

The Indians took one of these roads after they got far from the fort. They could travel more easily in it. They did not take pains to hide their tracks.

As fast as their feet could carry them, Boone and his friends traveled along the trail. When they had gone about ten miles they saw the Indians.

The Indians had stopped to rest and to eat. It was very warm and they had put off their moc-ca-sins and laid down their arms. They were kindling a fire to cook by.

In a moment the Indians saw the white men. Boone and Galloway were afraid the Indians would kill the girls.

Four of the white men shot at the Indians. Then all rushed at them.

The Indians ran away as fast as they could. They did not stop to pick up their guns or knives or hatchets. They had no time to put on their moccasins.

The poor worn-out girls were soon safe in their fathers' arms.

Back to Boones-bor-ough they went, not minding their tired feet. When they got to the fort there was great joy to see them alive.

I do not believe they ever played in the water again.

## *Decatur and the Pirates.*

Nearly a hundred years have passed since the ship "Phil-a-del-phi-a" was burned. But the brave sailors who did it will never be for-got-ten.

The people of Trip-o-li in Af-ri-ca were pirates. They took the ships of other nations at sea. They made slaves of their prisoners. The friends of these slaves sometimes sent money to buy their freedom. Some countries paid money to these pirates to let their ships go safe.

Our country had trouble with the pirates. This trouble brought on a war. Our ships were sent to fight against Trip-o-li.

One of the ships fighting against the pirates was called the "Phil-a-del-phi-a." One day she was chasing a ship of Trip-o-li. The "Phil-a-del-phi-a" ran on the rocks. The sailors could not get her off. The pirates came and fought her as she lay on the rocks. They took her men prisoners. Then they went to work to get her off. After a long time they got her into deep water. They took her to Tripoli. Our ships could not go there after her, because there were so many great cannons on the shore near the ship.

The pirates got the "Philadelphia" ready to go to sea. They loaded her cannons. They meant to slip out past our ships of war. Then they would take a great many smaller American ships.

But the Americans laid a plan to burn the "Philadelphia." It was a very dan-ger-ous thing to try to do. The pirates had ships of war near the "Philadelphia." They had great guns on the shore. There was no way to do it in the day-time. It could only be done by stealing into the Bay of Tripoli at night.

The Americans had taken a little vessel from the pirates. She was of the kind that is called a ketch. She had sails. She also had long oars. When there was no wind to sail with, the sailors could row her with the oars.

This little ketch was sent one night to burn the "Philadelphia." The captain of this boat was Ste-phen De-ca-tur. He was a young man, and very brave.

De-ca-tur made his men lie down, so that the pirates would not know how many men he had on his ketch. Only about ten men were in sight. The rest were lying hidden on the boat.

They came near to the "Philadelphia." It was about ten o'clock at night. The pirates called to them. The pilot of the ketch told them that he was from Mal-ta. He told them that he had come to sell things to the people of Tripoli. He said that the ketch had lost her anchor. He asked them to let him tie her to the big ship till morning.

The pirates sent out a rope to them. But when the ketch came nearer, the pirates saw that they had been fooled. They cried out, "Americans, Americans!"

Then the Americans lying down took hold of the rope and pulled with all their might, and drew the ketch close to the ship. They were so close, that the ship's cannons were over their heads. The pirates could not fire at them.

The men who had been lying still now rose up. There were eighty of them. In a minute they were scram-bling up the sides of the big ship. Some went in one way, some another. They did not shoot. They fought with swords and pikes, or short spears.

Soon they drove the pirates to one side of the ship. Then they could hear the pirates jumping over into the water. In a few minutes the pirates had all gone.

But the Americans could not stay long. They must burn the ship before the pirates on the shore should find out what they were doing.

They had brought a lot of kin-dling on the ketch. They built fires in all parts of the ship. The fire ran so fast, that some of the men had trouble to get off the ship.

When the Americans got back on the ketch, they could not untie the rope that held the ketch to the ship. The big ship was bursting into flames. The ketch would soon take fire.

They took swords and hacked the big rope in two. Then they pushed hard to get away from the fire. The ketch began to move. The sailors took the large oars and rowed. They were soon safe from the fire.

All this they had done without any noise. But, now that they had got away, they looked back. The fire was shooting up toward the sky. The men stopped rowing, and they gave three cheers. They were so glad, that they could not help it.

By this time the pirates on shore had waked up. They began to fire great cannon balls at the little ketch. One of the balls went through her sails. Ah! how the sailors rowed!

The whole sky was now lighted up by the fire. The pirates' cannons were thundering. The cannon balls were splashing the water all round the ketch. But the Americans got away. At last they were safe in their own ships.

## Stories About Jefferson.

Thomas Jef-fer-son was one of the great men of the Revolution. He was not a soldier. He was not a great speaker. But he was a great thinker. And he was a great writer.

He wrote a paper that was the very beginning of the United States. It was a paper that said that we would be free from England, and be a coun-try by our-selves. We call that paper the Dec-la-ra-tion of In-de-pend-ence.

When he was a boy, Jef-fer-son was fond of boyish plays. But when he was tired of play, he took up a book. It pleased him to learn things. From the time when he was a boy he never sat down to rest without a book.

At school he learned what other boys did. But the dif-fer-ence between him and most other boys was this: he did not stop with knowing just what the other boys knew. Most boys want to learn what other boys learn. Most girls would like to know what their school-mates know. But Jef-fer-son wanted to know a great deal more.

As a young man, Jefferson knew Latin and Greek. He also knew French and Span-ish and I-tal-ian.

He did not talk to show off what he knew. He tried to learn what other people knew. When he talked to a wagon maker, he asked him about such things as a wagon maker knows most about. He would sometimes ask how a wagon maker would go to work to make a wheel.

When Jefferson talked to a learn-ed man, he asked him about those things that this man knew most about. When he talked with Indians, he got them to tell him about their lan-guage. That is the way he came to know so much about so many things. Whenever anybody told him anything worth while, he wrote it down as soon as he could.

One day Jefferson was trav-el-ing. He went on horse-back. That was a common way of trav-el-ing at that time. He stopped at a country tavern. At this tavern he talked with a stranger who was staying there.

After a while Jefferson rode away. Then the stranger said to the land-lord, "Who is that man? He knew so much about law, that I was sure he was a lawyer. But when we talked about med-i-cine, he knew so much about that, that I thought he must be a doctor. And after a while he seemed to know so much about re-li-gion, that I was sure he was a min-is-ter. Who is he?"

The stranger was very much surprised to hear that the man he had talked with was Thomas Jefferson.

Jefferson was a very polite man. One day his grand-son was riding with him. They met a negro. The negro lifted his cap and bowed. Jefferson bowed to the negro. But his grand-son did not think it worth while to bow.

Then Jefferson said to his grand-son, "Do not let a poor negro be more of a gen-tle-man than you are."

In the Dec-la-ra-tion of In-de-pend-ence, Jefferson wrote these words: "All men are created equal." He also said that the poor man had the same right as the rich man to live, and to be free, and to try to make himself happy.

*A Long Journey.*

A long time ago, when Thomas Jefferson was Pres-i-dent, most of the people in this country lived in the East. Nobody knew anything about the Far West. The only people that lived there were Indians. Many of these Indians had never seen a white man.

An Elk.

The Pres-i-dent sent men to travel into this wild part of the country. He told them to go up to the upper end of the Mis-sou-ri River. Then they were to go across the Rocky Mountains. They were to keep on till they got to the Pa-cif-ic O-cean. Then they were to come back again. They were to find out the best way to get through the mountains. And they were to find out what kind of people the Indians in that country were. They were also to tell about the animals.

Feeding the Spirit of the Buffalo.

Edward Eggleston

There were two captains of this company. Their names were Lewis and Clark. There were forty-five men in the party.

They were gone two years and four months. For most of that time they did not see any white men but their own party. They did not hear a word from home for more than two years.

They got their food mostly by hunting. They killed a great many buf-fa-loes and elks and deer. They also shot wild geese and other large birds. Sometimes they had nothing but fish to eat. Sometimes they had to eat wolves. When they had no other meat, they were glad to buy dogs from the Indians and eat them. Sometimes they ate horses. They became fond of the meat of dogs and horses.

When they were very hungry, they had to live on roots if they could get them. Some of the Indians made a kind of bread out of roots. The white men bought this when they could not get meat. But there were days when they did not have anything to eat.

They were very friendly with the Indians. One day some of the men went to make a visit to an Indian village. The Indians gave them something to eat.

In the Indian wig-wam where they were, there was a head of a dead buffalo. When dinner was over, the Indians filled a bowl full of meat. They set this down in front of the head. Then they said to the head, "Eat that."

The Indians believed, that, if they treated this buffalo head politely, the live buffaloes would come to their hunting ground. Then they would have plenty of meat. They think the spirit of the buffalo is a kind of a god. They are very careful to please this god.

*Captain Clark's Burning Glass.*

The Indians among whom Captain Clark and Captain Lewis traveled had many strange ways of doing things. They had nothing like our matches for making fire. One tribe of Indians had this way of lighting a fire. An Indian would lay down a dry stick. He would rub this stick with the end of another stick. After a while this rubbing would make something like saw-dust on the stick that was lying down. The Indian would keep on rubbing till the wood grew hot. Then the fine wood dust would smoke. Then it would burn. The Indian would put a little kin-dling wood on it. Soon he would have a large fire.

In that time the white people had not yet found out how to make matches. They lighted a fire by striking a piece of flint against a piece of steel. This would make a spark of fire. By letting this spark fall on something that would burn easily, they started a fire.

White men had another way of lighting a fire when the sun was shining. They used what was called a burning glass. This was a round piece of glass. It was thick in the middle, and thin at the edge. When you held up a burning glass in the sun, it drew the sun's heat so as to make a little hot spot. If you put paper under this spot of hot sunshine, it would burn. Men could light the to-bac-co in their pipes with one of these glasses.

Captain Clark had something funny happen to him on account of his burning glass. He had walked ahead of the rest of his men. He sat down on a rock. There were some Indians on the other side of the river. They did not see the captain. Captain Clark saw a large bird called a crane flying over his head. He raised his gun and shot it.

Cranes.

The Indians on the other side of the river had never seen a white man in their lives. They had never heard a gun. They used bows and arrows.

They heard the sound of Clark's gun. They looked up and saw the large bird falling from the sky. It fell close to where Captain Clark sat. Just as it fell they caught sight of Captain Clark sitting on the rocks. They thought they had seen him fall out of the sky. They thought that the sound of his gun was a sound like thunder that was made when he came down.

The Indians all ran away as fast as they could. They went into their wig-warns and closed them.

Captain Clark wished to be friendly with them. So he got a canoe and paddled to the other side of the river. He came to the Indian houses. He found the flaps which they use for doors shut. He opened one of them and went in. The Indians were sitting down, and they were all crying and trembling.

Among the Indians the sign of peace is to smoke to-geth-er. Captain Clark held out his pipe to them. That was to say, "I am your friend." He shook hands with them and gave some of them presents. Then they were not so much afraid.

Lighting a Pipe with a Burning Glass.

He wished to light his pipe for them to smoke. So he took out his burning glass. He held it in the sun. He held his pipe under it. The sunshine was drawn together into a bright little spot on the tobacco. Soon the pipe began to smoke.

Then he held out his pipe for the Indians to smoke with him. That is their way of making friends. But none of the Indians would touch the pipe. They thought that he had brought fire down from heaven to light his pipe. They were now sure that he fell down from the sky. They were more afraid of him than ever.

At last Captain Clark's Indian man came. He told the other Indians that the white man did not come out of the sky. Then they smoked the pipe, and were not afraid.

*Quicksilver Bob.*

Robert Fulton was the man who set steam-boats to running on the rivers. Other men had made such boats before. But Fulton made the first good one.

When he was a boy, he lived in the town of Lan-cas-ter in Penn-syl-van-ia. Many guns were made in Lancaster. The men who made these guns put little pictures on them. That was to make them sell to the hunters who liked a gun with pictures. Little Robert Fulton could draw very well for a boy. He made some pretty little drawings. These the gun makers put on their guns.

Fulton went to the gun shops a great deal. He liked to see how things were made. He tried to make a small air gun for himself.

He was always trying to make things. He got some quick-sil-ver. He was trying to do something with it. But he would not tell what he wanted to do. So the gun-smiths called him Quick-sil-ver Bob.

He was so much in-ter-est-ed in such things, that he sometimes neg-lect-ed his lessons. He said that his head was so full of new notions, that he had not much room left for school learning.

One morning he came to school late.

"What makes you so late?" asked the teacher.

"I went to one of the shops to make myself a lead pencil," said little Bob. "Here it is. It is the best one I ever had."

The teacher tried it, and found it very good. Lead pencils in that day were made of a long piece of lead sharpened at the end.

Quick-sil-ver Bob was a very odd little boy. He said many cu-ri-ous things. Once the teacher punished him for not getting his lessons. He rapped Robert on the knuckles with a fer-ule. Robert did not like this any more than any other boy would.

"Sir," said the boy, "I came here to have something beaten into my head, not into my knuckles."

In that day people used to light candles and stand them in the window on the Fourth of July. These candles in every window lighted up the whole town. But one year candles were scarce and high. The city asked the people not to light up their windows on the Fourth.

Bob did not like to miss the fun of his Fourth of July. He went to work to make something like rockets or Roman candles. It was a very dan-ger-ous business for a boy.

"What are you doing, Bob?" some one asked him.

"The city does not want us to burn our candles on the Fourth," he said. "I am going to shoot mine into the air." He used to go fishing with a boy named Chris Gumpf. The father of Chris went with them. They fished from a flat boat. The two boys had to push the boat to the fishing place with poles.

"I am tired of poling that boat," said Robert to Chris one day when they came home.

So he set to work to think out a plan to move the boat in an easier way than by poles. He whittled out the model of a tiny paddle wheel. Then he went to work with Chris Gumpf, and they made a larger paddle wheel. This they set up in the fishing boat. The wheel was turned by the boys with a crank. They did not use the poles any more.

### The First Steamboat.

The first good steam-boat was built in New York. She was built by Robert Fulton. Her name was "Clermont." When the people saw her, they laughed. They said that such a boat would never go. For thousands of years boat-men had made their boats go by using sails and oars. People had never seen any such boat as this. It seemed foolish to believe that a boat could be pushed along by steam.

The time came for Fulton to start his boat. A crowd of people were standing on the shore. The black smoke was coming out of the smoke-stack. The people were laughing at the boat. They were sure that it would not go.

At last the boat's wheels began to turn round. Then the boat began to move. There were no oars. There were no sails. But still the boat kept moving. Faster and faster she went. All the people now saw that she could go by steam. They did not laugh any more. They began to cheer.

Seeing the First Steam boat.

The little steam-boat ran up to Al-ba-ny. The people who lived on the river did not know what to make of it. They had never heard of a steam-boat. They could not see what made the boat go.

There were many sailing vessels on the river. Fulton's boat passed some of these in the night. The sailors were afraid when they saw the fire and smoke. The sound of the steam seemed dreadful to them. Some of them went down-stairs in their ships for fear. Some of them went ashore. Perhaps they thought it was a living animal that would eat them up.

But soon there were steam-boats on all the large rivers.

*Washington Irving as a Boy.*

The Revolution was about over. Americans were very happy. Their country was to be free.

At this time a little boy was born in New York. His family was named Ir-ving. What should this little boy be named?

His mother said, "Washington's work is done. Let us name the baby Washington." So he was called Washington Ir-ving.

When this baby grew to be a little boy, he was one day walking with his nurse. The nurse was a Scotch girl. She saw General Washington go into a shop. She led the little boy into the shop also.

The nurse said to General Washington, "Please, your Honor, here is a bairn that is named for you."

"Bairn" is a Scotch word for child.

Washington put his hand on the little boy's head and gave him his blessing. When Irving became an author, he wrote a life of Washington.

Little Irving was a merry, playful boy. He was full of mischief.

Sometimes he would climb out of a window to the roof of his father's house. From this he would go to roofs of other houses. Then the little rascal would drop a pebble down a neighbor's chimney. Then he would hurry back and get into the window again. He would wonder what the people thought when the pebble came rattling down their chimney. Of course he was punished when his tricks were found out. But he was a favorite with his teacher. With all his faults, he would not tell a lie. The teacher called the little fellow "General."

Irving in Mischief.

In those days naughty school-boys were whipped. Irving could not bear to see another boy suffer. When a boy was to be whipped, the girls were sent out. Irving always asked the schoolmaster to let him go out with the girls.

Like other boys, Irving was fond of stories. He liked to read about Sind-bad the Sailor, and Rob-in-son Cru-soe. But most of all he liked to read about other countries. He had twenty small volumes called "The World Dis-played." They told about the people and countries of the world. Irving read these little books a great deal.

One day the schoolmaster caught him reading in school. The master slipped behind him and grabbed the book. Then he told Irving to stay after school.

Irving expected a pun-ish-ment. But the master told him he was pleased to find that he liked to read such good books. He told him not to read them in school.

Reading about other countries made Irving wish to see them. He thought he would like to travel. Like other wild boys, he thought of running away. He wanted to go to sea.

Rip Van Winkle wakes up.

But he knew that sailors had to eat salt pork. He did not like salt pork. He thought he would learn to like it. When he got a chance, he ate pork. And sometimes he would sleep all night on the floor. He wanted to get used to a hard bed.

But the more he ate pork, the more he disliked it. And the more he

*Edward Eggleston* 65

slept on the floor, the more he liked a good bed. So he gave up his foolish notion of being a sailor boy.

Some day you will read Irving's "Sketch Book." You will find some famous stories in it. There is the story of Rip Van Win-kle, who slept twenty years. And there is the funny story of the Head-less Horse-man. When you read these a-mus-ing stories, you will remember the playful boy who became a great author.

*Don't Give Up the Ship.*

Fred was talking to his sister one day. He said,—

"Alice, what makes people say, 'Don't give up the ship'?"

Alice said, "I don't know. That's what the teacher said to me yes-ter-day when I thought that I could not get my lesson."

"Yes," said Fred, "and that's what father said to me. I told him I never could learn to write well." He only said, "You must not give up the ship, my boy."

"I haven't any ship to give up," said Alice.

"And what has a ship to do with my writing?" said Fred.

"There must be some story about a ship," Alice said.

"Maybe grand-father would know," said Fred. "Let's ask him."

They found their grand-father writing in the next room. They did not wish to disturb him. They turned to leave the room.

But grand-father looked up just then. He smiled, and laid down his pen.

"Did you want something?" he asked.

"We wanted to ask you a question," said Alice. "We want to know why people say, 'Don't give up the ship.'"

"We thought maybe there is a story to it," said Fred.

"Yes, there is," said their grandfather. "And I know a little rhyme that tells the story."

"Could you say it to us?" asked Alice.

"Yes, if I can think of it. Let me see. How does it begin?"

Grandfather leaned his head back in the chair. He shut his eyes for a moment. He was trying to remember.

"Oh, now I remember it!" he said.

Then he said to them these little verses:—

*Grandfather's Rhyme.*

When I was but a boy,
  I heard the people tell
How gallant Captain Law-rence
  So bravely fought and fell.

The ships lay close together,
  I heard the people say,
And many guns were roaring
  Upon that battle day.

A grape-shot struck the captain,
  He laid him down to die:
They say the smoke of powder
  Made dark the sea and sky.

The sailors heard a whisper
  Upon the captain's lip:
The last command of Law-rence
  Was, "Don't give up the ship."

And ever since that battle
  The people like to tell
How gallant Captain Lawrence
  So bravely fought and fell.

When disappointment happens,
  And fear your heart annoys,
Be brave, like Captain Lawrence—
  And don't give up, my boys!

### The Star-Spangled Banner.

    Everybody in the United States has heard the song about the star-span-gled banner. Nearly everybody has sung it. It was written by Francis Scott Key.
    Key was a young lawyer. In the War of 1812 he fought with the American army. The British landed soldiers in Mary-land. At Bla-dens-burg they fought and beat the Americans. Key was in this battle on the American side.
    After the battle the British army took Washington, and burned the public buildings. Key had a friend who was taken prisoner by the British. He was on one of the British ships. Key went to the ships with a flag of truce. A flag of truce is a white flag. It is carried in war when one side sends a message to the other.
    When Key got to the British ships, they were sailing to Bal-ti-more. They were going to try to take Bal-ti-more. The British com-mand-er would not let Key go back. He was afraid that he would let the Americans know where the ships were going.
    Key was kept a kind of prisoner while the ships attacked Bal-ti-

more. The ships tried to take the city by firing at it from the water. The British army tried to take the city on the land side.

The ships did their worst firing at night. They tried to take the little fort near the city.

Key could see the battle. He watched the little fort. He was afraid that the men in it would give up. He was afraid that the fort would be broken down by the cannon balls.

The British fired bomb-shells and rockets at the fort. When these burst, they made a light. By this light Key could see that the little fort was still standing. He could see the flag still waving over it. He tells this in his song in these words:—

"And the rocket's red glare, the bombs bursting in air
Gave proof through the night that our flag was still there."

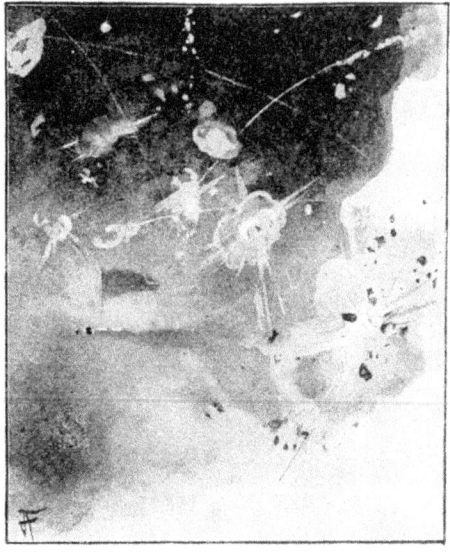

But after many hours of fighting the British became dis-cour-aged. They found that they could not take the city. The ships almost ceased to fire.

Key did not know whether the fort had been knocked down or not. He could not see whether the flag was still flying or not. He thought that the Americans might have given up. He felt what he wrote in the song:—

"Oh! say, does that star-span-gled banner yet wave
O'er the land of the free, and the home of the brave?"

When the break of day came, Key looked toward the fort. It was still standing. There was a flag flying over it. It grew lighter. He could see that it was the American flag. His feelings are told in two lines of the song:—

"Tis the star spangled banner, oh, long may it wave
O'er the land of the free, and the home of the brave!"

Key was full of joy. He took an old letter from his pocket. The back of this letter had no writing on it. Here he wrote the song about the star-spangled banner.

The British com-mand-er now let Key go ashore. When he got to Baltimore, he wrote out his song. He gave it to a friend. This friend took it to a printing office. But the printers had all turned soldiers. They had all gone to defend the city.

There was one boy left in the office. He knew how to print. He took the verses and printed them on a broad sheet of paper.

The printed song was soon in the hands of the soldiers around Baltimore. It was sung in the streets. It was sung in the the-a-ters. It traveled all over the country. Everybody learned to sing:—

"Then conquer we must, for our cause it is just;
And this be our motto—'In God is our trust'—
And the star-span-gled banner in triumph shall wave
O'er the land of the free, and the home of the brave."

## How Audubon Came to Know About Birds.

John James Au-du-bon knew more about the birds of this country than any man had ever known before. He was born in the State of Lou-is-i-a-na. His father took him to France when he was a boy. He went to school in France.

The little John James was fond of stud-y-ing about wild animals. But most of all he wished to know about birds. Seeing that the boy liked such things, his father took pains to get birds and flowers for him.

While he was yet a boy at school, he began to gather birds and other animals for himself. He learned to skin and stuff them. But his stuffed birds did not please him. Their feathers did not look bright, like those of live birds. He wanted living birds to study.

His father told him that he could not keep so many birds alive. To please the boy he got him a book with pictures in it. Looking at these pictures made John James wish to draw. He thought that he could make pictures that would look like the live birds.

But when he tried to paint a picture of a bird, it looked worse than his stuffed birds. The birds he drew were not much like real birds. He called them a "family of cripples." As often as his birthday came round, he made a bon-fire of his bad pictures. Then he would begin over again.

All this time he was learning to draw birds. But he was not willing to make pictures that were not just like the real birds. So when he grew to be a man he went to a great French painter whose name was David. David taught him to draw and paint things as they are.

Then he came back to this country, and lived awhile in Pennsylvania. Here his chief study was the wild creatures of the woods.

He gathered many eggs of birds. He made pictures of these eggs. He did not take birds' eggs to break up the nests. He was not cruel. He took only what he needed to study.

He would make two little holes in each egg. Then he would shake the egg, or stir it up with a little stick or straw, or a long pin. This would break up the inside of the egg. Then he would blow into one of the holes. That would blow the inside of the egg out through the other hole.

These egg shells he strung together by running strings through the holes. He hung these strings of egg shells all over the walls of his room. On the man-tel-piece he put the stuffed skins of squirrels, raccoons, o-pos-sums, and other small animals. On the shelves his friends could see frogs, snakes, and other animals.

He married a young lady, and brought her to live in this mu-se-um with his dead snakes, frogs, and strings of birds' eggs. She liked what he did, and was sure that he would come to be a great man.

He made up his mind to write a great book about American birds. He meant to tell all about the birds in one book. Then in another book he would print pictures of the birds, just as large as the birds themselves. He meant to have them look just like the birds.

To do this he must travel many thousands of miles. He must live for years almost all of the time in the woods. He would have to find and shoot the birds, in order to make pictures of them. And he must see how the birds lived, and how they built their nests, so that he could tell all about them. It would take a great deal of work and trouble. But he was not afraid of trouble.

That was many years ago. Much of our country was then covered with great trees. Au-du-bon sometimes went in a boat down a lonesome river. Sometimes he rode on horse-back. Often he had to travel on foot through woods where there were no roads. Many a time he had to sleep out of doors.

He lost his money and became poor. Sometimes he had to paint portraits to get money to live on. Once he turned dancing master for a while. But he did not give up his great idea. He still studied birds, and worked to make his books about American birds. His wife went to teaching to help make a living.

After years of hard work, he made paintings of nearly a thousand birds. That was almost enough for his books. But, while he was traveling, two large rats got into the box in which he kept his pictures. They cut up all his paintings with their teeth, and made a nest of the pieces. This almost broke his heart for a while. For many nights he could not sleep, because he had lost all his work.

But he did not give up. After some days he took his gun, and went into the woods. He said to himself, "I will begin over again. I can make better paintings than those that the rats spoiled." But it took him four long years and a half to find the birds, and make the pictures again.

He was so careful to have his drawings just like the birds, that he would measure them in every way. Thus he made his pictures just the size of the birds themselves.

At last the great books were printed. In this country, in France, and in England, people praised the won-der-ful books. They knew that Au-du-bon was indeed a great man.

Edward Eggleston

*Audubon in the Wild Woods.*

When Au-du-bon was making his great book about birds, he had to live much in the woods. Sometimes he lived among the Indians. He once saw an Indian go into a hollow tree. There was a bear in the tree. The Indian had a knife in his hand. He fought with the bear in the tree, and killed it.

Au-du-bon could shoot very well. A friend of his one day threw up his cap in the air. He told Au-du-bon to shoot at it. When the cap came down, it had a hole in it.

But the hunters who lived in the woods could shoot better. They would light a candle. Then one of the hunters would take his gun, and go a hundred steps away from the candle. He would then shoot at the candle. He would shoot so as to snuff it. He would not put out the candle. He would only cut off a bit of the wick with the bullet. But he would leave the candle burning.

Snuffing the Candle.

Once Audubon came near being killed by some robbers. He stopped at a cabin where lived an old white woman. He found a young Indian in the house. The Indian had hurt himself with an arrow. He had come to the house to spend the night.

The old woman saw Audubon's fine gold watch. She asked him to let her look at it. He put it into her hands for a minute. Then the Indian passed by Audubon, and pinched him two or three times. That was to let him know that the woman was bad, and that she might rob him.

Audubon went and lay down with his hand on his gun. After a while two men came in. They were the sons of the old woman. Then the old woman sharpened a large knife. She told the young men to kill the Indian first, and then to kill Audubon and take his watch. She thought that Audubon was asleep. But he drew up his gun ready to fire.

Just then two hunters came to the cabin. Audubon told them what the robbers were going to do. They took the old woman and her sons, and tied their hands and feet. The Indian, though he was in pain from his hurt, danced for joy when he saw that the robbers were caught. The woman and her sons were afterward punished.

### *Hunting a Panther.*

Audubon was traveling in the woods in Mis-sis-sip-pi. He found the little cabin of a settler. He staid there for the night. The settler told him that there was a panther in the swamp near his house. A panther is a very large and fierce animal. It is large enough to kill a man. This was a very bad panther. It had killed some of the settler's dogs.

Audubon said, "Let us hunt this panther, and kill it."

So the settler sent out for his neigh-bors to come and help kill the panther. Five men came. Audubon and the settler made seven. They were all on horse-back.

When they came to the edge of the swamp, each man went a dif-fer-ent way. They each took their dogs with them to find the track of the wild beast. All of the hunters carried horns. Who-ever should find the track first was to blow his horn to let the others know.

In about two hours after they had started, they heard the sound of a horn. It told them that the track had been found. Every man now went toward the sound of the horn. Soon all the yelping dogs were fol-low-ing the track of the fierce panther. The panther was running into the swamp farther and farther.

I suppose that the panther thought that there were too many dogs and men for him to fight. All the hunters came after the dogs. They held their guns ready to shoot if the panther should make up his mind to fight them.

After a while the sound of the dogs' voices changed. The hunters knew from this that the panther had stopped running, and gone up into a tree.

*Edward Eggleston*

At last the men came to the place where the dogs were. They were all barking round a tree. Far up in the tree was the dan-ger-ous beast. The hunters came up care-ful-ly. One of them fired. The bullet hit the panther, but did not kill him.

The panther sprang to the ground, and ran off again. The dogs ran after. The men got on their horses, and rode after.

But the horses were tired, and the men had to get down, and follow the dogs on foot.

The hunters now had to wade through little ponds of water. Sometimes they had to climb over fallen trees. Their clothes were badly torn by the bushes. After two hours more, they came to a place where the panther had again gone up into a tree.

This time three of the hunters shot at him. The fierce panther came tumbling to the ground. But he was still able to fight. The men fought the savage beast on all sides. At last they killed him. Then they gave his skin to the settler. They wanted him to know that his en-e-my was dead.

*Some Boys Who Became Authors.*

Wil-liam Cul-len Bry-ant was the first great poet in this country. He was a small man. When he was a baby, his head was too big for his body. His father used to send the baby to be dipped in a cold spring every day. The father thought that putting his head into cold water would keep it from growing.

Bry-ant knew his letters before he was a year and a half old. He began to write rhymes when he was a very little fellow. He wanted to be a poet. He used to pray that he might be a poet. His father printed some verses of his when he was only ten years old.

Bry-ant wrote many fine poems. Here are some lines of his about the bird we call a bob-o-link:—

> "Rob-ert of Lin-coln is gayly dressed,
>   Wearing a bright black wedding coat,
>  White are his shoulders and white his crest.
>   Hear him call in his merry note:
>    Bob-o'-link, bob-o'-link,
>    Spink, spank, spink;
>  Look, what a nice new coat is mine,
>  Sure there was never a bird so fine.
>    Chee, chee, chee.

Haw-thorne was one of our greatest writers of stories. He was a pretty boy with golden curls. He was fond of all the great poets, and he read Shake-speare and Mil-ton and many other poets as soon as he was old enough to un-der-stand them.

Haw-thorne grew up a very hand-some young fellow. One day he was walking in the woods. He met an old gypsy woman. She had never seen anybody so fine-looking.

"Are you a man, or an angel?" she asked him.

Some of Haw-thorne's best books are written for girls and boys. One of these is called "The Won-der Book." Another of his books for young people is "Tan-gle-wood Tales."

Pres-cott wrote beautiful his-to-ries. When Pres-cott was a boy, a school-mate threw a crust of bread at him. It hit him in the eye. He became almost blind.

He had to do his writing with a machine. This machine was made for the use of the blind. There were no type-writ-ers in those days.

It was hard work to write his-to-ry without good eyes. But Prescott did not give up. He had a man to read to him. It took him ten years to write his first book.

When Prescott had finished his book, he was afraid to print it. But his father said, "The man who writes a book, and is afraid to print it, is a cow-ard."

Then Prescott printed his book. Everybody praised it. When you are older, you will like to read his his-to-ries.

Doctor Holmes, the poet, was a boy full of fancies. He lived in an old house. Soldiers had staid in the house at the time of the Revolution. The floor of one room was all battered by the butts of the soldiers' muskets.

Little Ol-i-ver Holmes used to think he could hear soldiers in the house. He thought he could hear their spurs rattling in the dark passages. Sometimes he thought he could hear their swords clanking.

The little boy was afraid of a sign that hung over the sidewalk. It was a great, big, wooden hand. It was the sign of a place where gloves were made. This big hand swung in the air. Little Ol-i-ver Holmes had to walk under it on his way to school. He thought the great fingers would grab him some day. Then he thought he would never get home again. He even thought that his other pair of shoes would be put away till his little brother grew big enough to wear them.

But the big wooden hand never caught him.

Here are some verses that Doctor Holmes wrote about a very old man:—

"My grand-mam-ma has said—
 Poor old lady, she is dead
  Long ago—
 That he had a Roman nose,
 And his cheek was like a rose
  In the snow.

"But now his nose is thin,
 And it rests upon his chin
  Like a staff;
 And a crook is in his back,
 And a mel-an-chol-y crack
  In his laugh.

"I know it is a sin
 For me to sit and grin
  At him here;
 But the old three-cor-nered hat,
 And the breeches, and all that,
  Are so queer!

"And if I should live to be
The last leaf upon the tree
In the spring,
Let them smile, as I do now,
At the old for-sak-en bough
Where I cling."

*Daniel Webster and His Brother.*

Dan-iel Web-ster was a great states-man. As a little boy he was called "Little Black Dan." When he grew larger, he was thin and sickly-looking. But he had large, dark eyes. People called him "All Eyes."

He was very fond of his brother E-ze-ki-el. E-ze-ki-el was a little older than Dan-iel. Both the boys had fine minds. They wanted to go to college. But their father was poor.

Dan-iel had not much strength for work on the farm. So little "All Eyes" was sent to school, and then to college. E-ze-ki-el staid at home, and worked on the farm.

While Daniel was at school, he was unhappy to think that Ezekiel could not go to college also. He went home on a visit. He talked to Ezekiel about going to college. The brothers talked about it all night.

The next day Daniel talked to his father about it. The father said he was too poor to send both of his sons to college. He said he would lose all his little property if he tried to send Ezekiel to college. But he said, that, if their mother and sisters were willing to be poor, he would send the other son to college.

So the mother and sisters were asked. It seemed hard to risk the loss of all they had. It seemed hard not to give Ezekiel a chance. They all shed tears over it.

The boys promised to take care of their mother and sisters if the property should be lost. Then they all agreed that Ezekiel should go to college too.

Daniel taught school while he was studying. That helped to pay the expenses. After Daniel was through with his studies in college, he taught a school in order to help his brother. When his school closed, he went home. On his way he went round to the college to see his brother. Finding that Ezekiel needed money, he gave him a hundred dollars. He kept but three dollars to get home with.

The father's property was not sold. The two boys helped the family. Daniel soon began to make money as a lawyer. He knew that his father was in debt. He went home to see him.

He said, "Father, I am going to pay your debts."

The father said, "You cannot do it, Daniel. You have not money enough."

"I can do it," said Daniel; "and I will do it before Monday evening."

When Monday evening came round, the father's debts were all paid.

When Daniel became a famous man, it made Ezekiel very happy. But Ezekiel died first. When Daniel Web-ster made his greatest speech, all the people praised him.

But Web-ster said, "I wish that my poor brother had lived to this time. It would have made him very happy."

Webster and the Poor Woman.

*Edward Eggleston*

## Webster and the Poor Woman.

When Daniel Webster was a young lawyer, he was going home one night. There was snow on the ground. It was very cold. It was late, and there was nobody to be seen.

But after a while he saw a poor woman. She was ahead of him. He wondered what had brought her out on so cold a night.

Sometimes she stopped and looked around. Then she would stand and listen. Then she would go on again.

Webster kept out of her sight. But he watched her. After looking around, she turned down the street in which Webster lived. She stopped in front of Webster's house. She looked around and listened.

Webster had put down some loose boards to walk on. They reached from the gate to the door of his house. After standing still a minute, the woman took one of the boards, and went off quickly.

Webster followed her. But he kept out of her sight. She went to a distant part of the town. She went into a poor little house.

Webster went home without saying anything to the woman. He knew that she had stolen the board for fire-wood.

The next day the poor woman got a present It was a nice load of wood.

Can you guess who sent it to her?

## The India-Rubber Man.

Many years ago a strange-looking man was sometimes seen in the streets of New York. His cap was made of In-di-a rubber. So was his coat. He wore a rubber waist-coat. Even his cravat was of In-di-a rubber. He wore rubber shoes in dry weather. People called this man "The In-di-a-rubber man."

His name was Charles Good-year. He was very poor. He was trying to find out how to make India rubber useful.

India-rubber trees grow in South America. The juice of these trees is something like milk or cream. By drying this juice, India rubber is made.

The Indians in Bra-zil have no glass to make bottles with. A long time ago they learned to make bottles out of rubber. More than a hundred years ago some of these rubber bottles were brought to this country. The people in this country had never seen India rubber before. They thought the bottles made out of it by the Indians very cu-ri-ous.

In this country, rubber was used only to rub out pencil marks. That is why we call it rubber. People in South America learned to make a kind of heavy shoe out of it. But these shoes were hard to make. They cost a great deal when they were sold in this country.

Men tried to make rubber shoes in this country. They got the rubber from Bra-zil. Rubber shoes made in this country were cheaper than those brought from South America. But they were not good. They would freeze till they were as hard as stones in winter. That was not the worst of it. In summer they would melt.

Goodyear was trying to find out a way to make rubber better. He wanted to get it so that it would not melt in summer. He wanted to get a rubber that would not get hard in cold weather. The first rubber coats that were made were so hard in cold weather, that they would stand alone, and look like a man.

Goodyear wanted to try his rubber. That is why he wore a rubber coat and a rubber waist-coat and a rubber cravat. That is why he wore a rubber cap and rubber shoes when it was not raining. He made paper out of rubber, and wrote a book on it. He had a door-plate made of it. He even carried a cane made of India rubber. It is no wonder people called him the India-rubber man.

He was very poor. Sometimes he had to borrow money to buy rubber with. Sometimes his friends gave him money to keep his family from starving. Sometimes there was no wood and no coal in the house in cold weather.

But Goodyear kept on trying. He thought that he was just going to find out. Years went by, and still he kept on trying.

One day he was mixing some rubber with sulphur. It slipped out of his hand. It fell on the hot stove. But it did not melt. Goodyear was happy at last.

That night it was cold. Goodyear took the burned piece of rubber out of doors, and nailed it to the kitchen door. When morning came, he went and got it. It had not frozen.

He was now sure that he was on the right track. But he had to find out how to mix and heat his rubber and sulphur. He was too poor to buy rubber to try with. Nobody would lend him any more money. His family had to live by the help of his friends. He had already sold almost everything that he had. Now he had to sell his children's school-books to get money to buy rubber with.

At last his rubber goods were made and sold. Poor men who had to stand in the rain could now keep themselves dry. People could walk in the wet with dry feet. A great many people are alive who would have died if they had not been kept dry by India rubber.

You may count up, if you can, how many useful things are made of rubber. We owe them all to one man. People laughed at Goodyear once. But at last they praised him. To be "The India-rubber man" was something to be proud of.

*Doctor Kane in the Frozen Sea.*

Kane was a doctor in one of the war ships of the United States. He had sailed about the world a great deal.

When he heard that ships were to be sent into the icy seas of the north, he asked to be sent along. He went the first time as a doctor. Then he wanted to find out more about the frozen ocean. So he went again as captain of a ship. His ship was called the "Advance."

Kane sailed into the icy seas. His ship was driven far into the ice by a fu-ri-ous storm. She was crowded by ice-bergs. At one time she was lifted clear out of the water. The ship seemed ready to fall over on her side. But the ice let her down again. Then she was squeezed till the men thought that she would be crushed like an egg shell.

At last the storm stopped. Then came the awful cold. The ship was frozen into the ice. The ice never let go of her. She was farther north than any ship had ever been before. But she was so fast in the ice that she never could get away.

In that part of the world it is night nearly all winter. For months there was no sun at all. Daylight came again. It was now summer, but it did not get warm. Doctor Kane took sleds, and went about on the ice to see what he could see. The sleds were drawn by large dogs. But nearly all of the dogs died in the long winter night.

A Dog Sled.

Doctor Kane thought that the ice would melt. He wanted to get the ship out. But the ice did not melt at all.

At last the summer passed away. Another awful winter came. The sun did not rise any more. It was dark for months and months. The men were ill. Some of them died. They were much dis-cour-aged. But Kane kept up his heart, and did the best he could.

At last the least little streak of light could be seen. It got a little lighter each day. But the sick men down in the cabin of the ship could not see the light.

Doctor Kane said to himself, "If my poor men could see this sunlight, it would cheer them up. It might save their lives." But they were too ill to get out where they could see the sun. It would be many days before the sun would shine into the cabin of the ship. The men might die before that time.

So Doctor Kane took some looking glasses up to the deck or top of the ship. He fixed one of these so it would catch the light of the sun. Then he fixed another so that the first one would throw the light on this one. The last one would throw the sunlight down into the cabin where the sick men were.

One day the poor fellows were ready to give up. Then the sun fell on the looking glasses, and flashed down into the cabin. It was the first daylight the sick men had seen for months. The long winter night was over. Think how happy they were!

## A DINNER ON THE ICE.

After two winters of cold and darkness, Doctor Kane made up his mind to leave the ship fast in the ice. He wanted to get to a place in Green-land where there were people living. Then he might find some way of getting home again.

The men started out, drawing the boats on sleds. Whenever they came to open water, they put the boats into the water, and took the sleds in the boats. When they came to the ice again, they had to draw out their boats, and carry them on the sleds. At first they could travel only about a mile a day.

It was a hard journey. Some of the men were ill. These had to be drawn on the sleds by the rest. They had not enough food. At one time they rested three days in a kind of cave. Here they found many birds' eggs. These made very good food for them. At another place they staid a week. They staid just to eat the eggs of the wild birds.

After they left this place, they were hungry. The men grew thinner and thinner. It seemed that they must die for want of food. But one day they saw a large seal. He was floating on a piece of ice. The hungry men thought, "What a fine din-ner he would make for us!" If they could get the seal, they would not die of hunger.

Every one of the poor fellows trembled for fear the seal would wake up. A man named Pe-ter-sen took a gun, and got ready to shoot. The men rowed the boat toward the seal. They rowed slowly and quietly. But the seal waked up. He raised his head. The men thought that he would jump off into the water. Then they might all die for want of food.

Doctor Kane made a motion to Pe-ter-sen. That was to tell him to shoot quickly. But Peter-sen did not shoot. He was so much afraid that the seal would get away, that he could not shoot. The seal now raised himself a little more. He was getting ready to jump into the water. Just then Petersen fired. The seal fell dead on the ice.

A Seal.

The men were wild with joy. They rowed the boats with all their might. When they got to the seal, they dragged it farther away from the water. They were so happy, that they danced on the ice. Some of them laughed. Some were so glad, that they cried.

Shooting the Seal.

Then they took their knives and began to cut up the seal. They had no fire on the ice, and they were too hungry to think of lighting one. So they ate the meat of the seal without waiting to cook it.

### Doctor Kane Gets Out of the Frozen Sea.

After they got the seal, Doctor Kane and his men traveled on. Sometimes they were on the ice. Sometimes they were in the boats. The men were so weak, that they could hardly row the boats. They were so hungry, that they could not sleep well at night.

One day they were rowing, when they heard a sound. It came to them across the water. It did not sound like the cry of sea birds. It sounded like people's voices.

"Listen!" Doctor Kane said to Pe-ter-sen.

Petersen spoke the same language as the people of Greenland. He listened. The sound came again. Pe-ter-sen was so glad, that he could hardly speak. He told Kane in a half whisper, that it was the voice of some one speaking his own language. It was some Greenland men in a boat.

The next day they got to a Greenland town. Then they got into a little ship going to England. They knew that they could get home from England. But the ship stopped at another Green-land town. While they were there, a steamer was seen. It came nearer. They could see the stars and stripes flying from her mast. It was an American steamer sent to find Doctor Kane.

Doctor Kane and his men were full of joy. They pushed their little boat into the water once more. This little boat was called the "Faith." It had carried Kane and his men hundreds of miles in icy seas.

Once more the men took their oars, and rowed. This time they rowed with all their might. They held up the little flag that they had carried farther north than anybody had ever been before. They rowed straight to the steamer.

In the bow of the boat was a little man with a tattered red shirt. He could see that the captain of the boat was looking at him through a spy-glass.

The captain shouted to the little man, "Is that Doctor Kane?"

The little man in the red shirt shouted back, "Yes!"

Doctor Kane and his men had been gone more than two years. People had begun to think that they had all died. This steamer had been sent to find out what had become of them. When the men on the steamer heard that this little man in the red shirt was Doctor Kane himself, they sent up cheer after cheer.

In a few minutes more, Doctor Kane and his men were on the steamer. They were now safe among friends. They were sailing away toward their homes.

*Longfellow as a Boy.*

Long-fel-low was a noble boy. He always wanted to do right. He could not bear to see one person do any wrong to another.

He was very tender-hearted. One day he took a gun and went shooting. He killed a robin. Then he felt sorry for the robin He came home with tears in his eyes. He was so grieved, that he never went shooting again.

He liked to read Irving's "Sketch Book." Its strange stories about Sleepy Hollow and Rip Van Win-kle pleased his fancy.

When he was thirteen he wrote a poem. It was about Love-well's fight with the Indians. He sent his verses to a news-paper. He wondered if the ed-i-tor would print them. He could not think of anything else. He walked up and down in front of the printing office. He thought that his poem might be in the printer's hands.

Longfellow and the Bird.

When the paper came out, there was his poem. It was signed "Henry." Long-fel-low read it. He thought it a good poem.

But a judge who did not know whose poem it was talked about it that evening. He said to young Long-fel-low, "Did you see that poem in the paper? It was stiff. And all taken from other poets, too."

This made Henry Long-fel-low feel bad. But he kept on trying. After many years, he became a famous poet.

For more than fifty years, young people have liked to read his poem called "A Psalm of Life." Here are three stanzas of it:—

> "Lives of great men all remind us
>     We can make our lives sub-lime,
> And, de-part-ing, leave behind us
>     Foot-prints on the sands of time,—

> "Foot-prints, that perhaps another,
> Sailing o'er life's solemn main,
> A forlorn and ship-wrecked brother,
> Seeing, may take heart again.
>
> "Let us, then, be up and doing,
> With a heart for any fate;
> Still a-chiev-ing, still pur-su-ing,
> Learn to labor and to wait."

### Kit Carson and the Bears.

Great men of one kind are known only in new countries like ours. These men dis-cov-er new regions. They know how to manage the Indians. They show other people how to live in a wild country.

One of the most famous of such men was Kit Car-son. He knew all about the wild animals. He was a great hunter. He learned the languages of the Indians. The Indians liked him. He was a great guide. He showed soldiers and settlers how to travel where they wished to go.

Once he was marching through the wild country with other men. Evening came. He left the others, and went to shoot something to eat. It was the only way to get meat for supper.

When he had gone about a mile, he saw the tracks of some elks. He followed these tracks. He came in sight of the elks. They were eating grass on a hill, as cows do.

Kit Car-son crept up behind some bushes. But elks are very timid animals. Before the hunter got very near, they began to run away. So Carson fired at one of them as it was running. The elk fell dead.

But just at that moment he heard a roar. He turned to see what made this ugly noise. Two huge bears were running toward him. They wanted some meat for supper, too.

Kit Carson's gun was empty. He threw it down. Then he ran as fast as he could. He wanted to find a tree.

Just as the bears were about to seize him, he got to a tree. He caught hold of a limb. He swung himself up into the tree. The bears just missed getting him.

But bears know how to climb trees. Carson knew that they would soon be after him. He pulled out his knife, and began to cut off a limb. He wanted to make a club.

A bear is much larger and stronger than a man. He cannot be killed with a club. But every bear has one tender spot. It is his nose. He does not like to be hit on the nose. A sharp blow on the nose hurts him a great deal.

Kit Carson got his club cut just in time. The bears were coming after him. Kit got up into the very top of the tree. He drew up his feet, and made himself as small as he could.

When the bears came near, one of them reached for Kit. Whack! went the stick on the end of his nose. The bear drew back, and whined with pain.

First one bear tried to get him, and then the other. But which-ever one tried, Kit was ready. The bear was sure to get his nose hurt.

The bears grew tired, and rested awhile. But they kept up their screeching and roaring. When their noses felt better, they tried again. And then they tried again. But every time they came away with sore noses.

At last they both tried at once. But Carson pounded faster than ever. One of the bears cried like a baby. The tears ran out of his eyes. It hurt his feelings to have his nose treated in this rude way.

After a long time one of the bears got tired. He went away. After awhile the other went away too. Kit Carson staid in the tree a long time. Then he came down. The first thing he did was to get his gun. He loaded it. But the bears did not come back. They were too busy rubbing noses.

## Horace Greeley as a Boy.

Hor-ace Gree-ley was the son of a poor farmer. He was always fond of books. He learned to read almost as soon as he could talk. He could read easy books when he was three years old. When he was four, he could read any book that he could get.

He went to an old-fashioned school. Twice a day all the children stood up to spell. They were in two classes. Little Hor-ace was in the class with the grown-up young people. He was the best speller in the class. It was funny to see the little midget at the head of this class of older people.

But he was only a little boy in his feelings. If he missed a word, he would cry. The one that spelled a word that he missed would have a right to take the head of the class. Sometimes when he missed, the big boys would not take the head. They did not like to make the little fellow cry. He was the pet of all the school.

People in that day were fond of spelling. They used to hold meetings at night to spell. They called these "spelling schools."

At a spelling school two captains were picked out. These chose their spellers. Then they tried to see which side could beat the other at spelling.

Greeley Reading.

Little Hor-ace was always chosen first. The side that got him got the best speller in the school. Sometimes the little fellow would go to sleep. When it came his turn to spell, some-body would wake him up. He would rub his eyes, and spell the word. He would spell it right, too.

When he was four or five years old, he would lie under a tree, and read. He would lie there, and forget all about his dinner or his supper. He would not move until some-body stumbled over him or called him.

People had not found out how to burn ker-o-sene oil in lamps then. They used candles. But poor people like the Gree-leys could not afford to burn many candles. Hor-ace gathered pine knots to read by at night.

He would light a pine knot Then he would throw it on top of the large log at the back of the fire. This would make a bright flick-er-ing light.

Horace would lay all the books he wanted on the hearth. Then he would lie down by them. His head was toward the fire. His feet were drawn up out of the way.

The first thing that he did was to study all his lessons for the next day. Then he would read other books. He never seemed to know when anybody came or went. He kept on with his reading. His father did not want him to read too late. He was afraid that he would hurt his eyes. And he wanted to have him get up early in the morning to help with the work. So when nine o'clock came, he would call, "Horace, Horace, Horace!" But it took many callings to rouse him.

When he got to bed, he would say his lessons over to his brother. He would tell his brother what he had been reading. But his brother would fall asleep while Horace was talking.

Horace liked to read better than he liked to work. But when he had a task to do, he did it faith-ful-ly. His brother would say, "Let us go fishing." But Horace would answer, "Let us get our work done first."

Horace Gree-ley's father grew poorer and poorer. When Horace was ten years old, his land was sold. The family were now very poor. They moved from New Hamp-shire. They settled in Ver-mont. They lived in a poor little cabin.

Horace had to work hard like all the rest of the family. But he borrowed all the books he could get. Sometimes he walked seven miles to borrow a book.

A rich man who lived near the Greeleys used to lend books to Horace. Horace had grown tall. His hair was white. He was poorly dressed. He was a strange-looking boy.

One day he went to the house of the rich man to borrow books. Some one said to the owner of the house, "Do you lend books to such a fellow as that?"

But the gen-tle-man said, "That boy will be a great man some day."

This made all the com-pa-ny laugh. It seemed funny that anybody

Edward Eggleston

should think of this poor boy becoming a great man. But it came true. The poor white-headed boy came to be a great man.

Horace Greeley learned all that he could learn in the country schools.

When he was thirteen, one teacher said to his father,—

"Mr. Greeley, Horace knows more than I do. It is not of any use to send him to school any more."

### Horace Greeley Learning to Print.

Horace Greeley had always wanted to be a printer. He liked books and papers. He thought it would be a fine thing to learn to make them.

One day he heard that the news-paper at East Poult-ney wanted a boy to learn the printer's trade. He walked many long miles to see about it. He went to see Mr. Bliss. Mr. Bliss was one of the owners of the paper. Horace found him working in his garden.

Mr. Bliss looked up. He saw a big boy coming toward him. The boy had on a white felt hat with a narrow brim. It looked like a half-peck measure. His hair was white. His trousers were too short for him. All his clothes were coarse and poor. He was such a strange-looking boy, that Mr. Bliss wanted to laugh.

"I heard that you wanted a boy," Horace said.

"Do you want to learn to print?" Mr. Bliss said.

"Yes," said Horace.

"But a printer ought to know a good many things," said Mr. Bliss. "Have you been to school much?"

"No," said Horace. "I have not had much chance at school. But I have read some."

"What have you read?" asked Mr. Bliss.

"Well, I have read some his-to-ry, and some travels, and a little of everything."

Mr. Bliss had ex-am-ined a great many schoolteachers. He liked to puzzle teachers with hard questions. He thought he would try Horace with these. But the gawky boy answered them all. This tow-headed boy seemed to know everything.

Mr. Bliss took a piece of paper from his pocket. He wrote on it, "Guess we'd better try him."

He gave this paper to Horace, and told him to take it to the printing office. Horace, with his little white hat and strange ways, went into the printing office. The boys in the office laughed at him. But the foreman said he would try him.

That night the boys in the office said to Mr. Bliss, "You are not going to take that tow head, are you?"

Mr. Bliss said, "There is something in that tow-head. You boys will find it out soon."

Greeley setting Type.

A few days after this, Horace came to East Poult-ney to begin his work. He carried a little bundle of clothes tied up in a hand-ker-chief.

The fore-man showed him how to begin. From that time he did not once look around. All day he worked at his type. He learned more in a day than some boys do in a month.

Day after day he worked, and said nothing. The other boys joked him. But he did not seem to hear them. He only kept on at his work. They threw type at him. But he did not look up.

The largest boy in the office thought he could find a way to tease him. One day he said that Horace's hair was too white. He went and got the ink ball. He stained Horace's hair black in four places. This ink stain would not wash out. But Horace did not once look up.

After that, the boys did not try to tease him any more. They all liked the good-hearted Horace. And everybody in the town wondered that the boy knew so much.

Horace's father had moved away to Penn-syl-va-ni-a. Horace sent him all the money he could spare. He soon became a good printer. He started a paper of his own. He became a famous news-paper man.

## A Wonderful Woman.

Little Dor-o-thy Dix was poor. Her father did not know how to make a living. Her mother did not know how to bring up her children.

The father moved from place to place. Sometimes he printed little tracts to do good. But he let his own children grow up poor and wretched.

Dor-o-thy wanted to learn. She wanted to become a teacher. She wanted to get money to send her little brothers to school.

Dor-o-thy was a girl of strong will and temper. When she was twelve years old, she left her wretched home. She went to her grand-mother. Her grand-mother Dix lived in a large house in Boston. She sent Dorothy to school.

Dorothy learned fast. But she wanted to make money. She wanted to help her brothers. When she was fourteen, she taught a school. She tried to make herself look like a woman. She made her dresses longer.

She soon went back to her grand-mother. She went to school again. Then she taught school. She soon had a school in her grandmother's house. It was a very good school. Many girls were sent to her school.

Miss Dix was often ill. But when she was well enough, she worked away. She was able to send her brothers to school until they grew up.

Besides helping her brothers, she wanted to help other poor children. She started a school for poor children in her grandmother's barn.

After a while she left off teaching. She was not well. She had made all the money she needed.

But she was not idle. She went one day to teach some poor women in an alms-house. Then she went to see the place where the crazy people were kept. These insane people had no fire in the coldest weather.

Miss Dix tried to get the man-a-gers to put up a stove in the room. But they would not do it. Then she went to the court. She told the judge about it. The judge said that the insane people ought to have a fire. He made the man-a-gers put up a stove in the place where they were kept.

Then Miss Dix went to other towns. She wanted to see how the insane people were treated. Some of them were shut up in dark, damp cells. One young man was chained up with an iron collar about his neck.

Miss Dix got new laws made about the insane. She per-suad-ed the States to build large houses for keeping the insane. She spent most of her life at this work.

The Civil War broke out. There were many sick and wounded soldiers to be taken care of.

All of the nurses in the hos-pi-tals were put under Miss Dix. She worked at this as long as the war lasted. Then she spent the rest of her life doing all that she could for insane people.

## The Author of "Little Women."

Lou-i-sa Al-cott was a wild little girl. When she was very little, she would run away from home. She liked to play with beggar children.

One day she wandered so far away from her home, she could not find the way back again. It was growing dark. The little girl's feet were tired. She sat down on a door-step. A big dog was lying on the step. He wagged his tail. That was his way of saying, "I am glad to see you."

Little Lou-i-sa grew sleepy. She laid her head on the curly head of the big dog. Then she fell asleep.

Lou-i-sa's father and mother could not find her. They sent out the town crier to look for her.

The town crier went along the street. As he went, he rang his bell. Every now and then he would tell that a little girl was lost.

At last the man with the bell came to the place where Louisa was asleep. He rang his bell. That waked her up. She heard him call out in a loud voice,—

"Lost, lost! a little girl six years old. She wore a pink frock, a white hat, and new green shoes."

When the crier had said that, he heard a small voice coming out of the darkness. It said, "Why, dat's me." The crier went to the voice, and found Louisa sitting by the big dog on the door-step. The next day she was tied to the sofa to punish her for running away.

She and her sisters learned to sew well. Louisa set up as a doll's dress-maker. She was then twelve years old. She hung out a little sign. She put some pretty dresses in the window to show how well she could do.

Other girls liked the little dresses that she made. They came to her to get dresses made for their dolls. They liked the little doll's hats she made better than all. Louisa chased the chickens to get soft feathers for these hats.

She turned the old fairy tales into little plays. The children played these plays in the barn.

One of these plays was Jack and the Bean-stalk. A squash vine was put up in the barn. This was the bean-stalk. When it was cut down, the boy who played giant would come tumbling out of the hay-loft.

Louisa found it hard to be good and o-be-di-ent. She wrote some verses about being good. She was fourteen years old when she wrote them. Here they are:—

### My Kingdom.

A little kingdom I possess
　Where thoughts and feelings dwell,
And very hard I find the task
　Of gov-ern-ing it well.

For passion tempts and troubles me,
　A wayward will misleads,
And sel-fish-ness its shadow casts
　On all my words and deeds.

I do not ask for any crown
　But that which all may win,
Nor seek to conquer any world
　Except the one within.

The Al-cott family were very poor. Louisa made up her mind to do something to make money when she got big. She did not like being so very poor.

One day she was sitting on a cart-wheel thinking. She was thinking how poor her father was. There was a crow up in the air over her head. The crow was cawing. There was nobody to tell her thoughts to but the crow. She shook her fist at the big bird, and said,—

"I will do something by and by. Don't care what. I'll teach, sew, act, write, do anything to help the family. And I'll be rich and famous before I die. See if I don't."

The crow did not make any answer. But Louisa kept thinking about the work she was going to do. The other children got work to do that made money. But Louisa was left at home to do housework. She had to do the washing. She made a little song about it. Here are some of the verses of this song:—

*A Song From the Suds.*

Queen of my tub, I merrily sing,
    While the white foam rises high,
And stur-di-ly wash and rinse and wring,
    And fasten the clothes to dry;
Then out in the free fresh air they swing,
    Under the sunny sky.

I am glad a task to me is given,
    To labor at day by day;
For it brings me health and strength and hope,
    And I cheer-ful-ly learn to say,
"Head you may think, Heart you may feel,
    But Hand you shall work alway."

Louisa grew to be a woman at last. She went to nurse soldiers in the war. She wrote books. When she wrote the book called "Little Women," all the young people were de-light-ed. What she had said to the crow came true at last. She became famous. She had money enough to make the family com-fort-a-ble.

THE END

www.ingramcontent.com/pod-product-compliance
Lightning Source LLC
Chambersburg PA
CBHW031411040426
42444CB00005B/522